ACROSS
1. Pronoun
4. Grouchy person
8. Highest mountain in Canada
13. Orgs. for concerned parents
14. In good health
15. Deteriorate
16. Assam silkworms
17. Dog in *The Thin Man*
18. Not hollow
19. Polo and skiing
22. Overimbiber's woe
23. Musical instrument
24. Sows
26. Numerical prefix
29. Nostril titillaters
32. Cheryl and Alan
36. Fills with wonderment
38. Vermin
39. Tribal member
40. Spot
41. Esse or estar, in French
42. Chickens
43. Mideast bigwig
44. Pale
45. Like a circus
47. U-__
49. Parties
51. Marie or Donny Osmond
56. Taxing time: abbr.
58. Organize like Webster did
61. Smallest
63. Actor Julia
64. Burden
65. Tune from the past
66. Island republic
67. North and Mediterranean, to a Parisian
68. SAT takers, often
69. Paleozoic and Mesozoic
70. Traveler's direction: abbr.

DOWN
1. Ascending parts
2. Poorest western nation
3. City located 18 miles northeast of Düsseldorf
4. Virginal
5. Scrape
6. Quartet member
7. Endures
8. *Children of a __ God;* 1986 Best Actress' film
9. Valuable ore, in Valencia
10. Novelist Oliver (1730-74)
11. Underground passage
12. Sparks and Beatty
13. Seats for many
20. Colors
21. Rib
25. Concave roofs
27. Relaxed
28. Anticipate
30. Measurement
31. Noticed
32. Section of a barn
33. Stub __ ; stumble while barefoot
34. Demote
35. Triangular river deposit
37. One of the earth tones
40. Propel a bike
44. Prefix for room or date
46. Raises the spirits of
48. Foreign currency
50. Fling
52. Tiny bits
53. Jazz pianist Earl
54. Blue
55. Suffix for glad or sad
56. Much
57. Brazilian athlete
59. Long-running Broadway musical
60. Invisible emanation
62. Do wrong

HOURS OF ENJOYMENT!

CROSSWORD

PUZZLES

PACKED WITH CHALLENGING PUZZLES!

VOLUME

32

ACROSS

1. Bikini part
6. Sound the horn
10. Saw
14. Babble
15. Oriental nursemaid
16. Yokel
17. Portrait support
18. Lunch spot
20. Napoleon or Hirohito: abbr.
21. Den
23. Let up
24. Impudent
25. Degree pursuer
27. Give
30. Fellow
31. Draft board: abbr.
34. Fail to include
35. Fry
36. __ degree; somewhat
37. Famous 1936 ballet
41. Wind dir.
42. Venerate
43. Lifted with effort
44. Former Soviet div.
45. Mere's partner
46. Handbooks
48. Fuzzy stuff
49. Dispatched
50. Shaw
53. Common contraction
54. Food fish
57. Film container
60. Market of old
62. Level
63. Before long
64. Want ardently
65. __ fixe
66. Sandwich
67. Water-retention problem

DOWN

1. Graf __
2. Public transport
3. Scrape
4. Feasted
5. Lead shot
6. Implied
7. Poet Khayyam
8. Nincompoop
9. Article
10. Trample
11. Pronoun
12. Actor's award
13. Pioneer
19. Structure made of animal pelts: var.
22. Common verb
24. Cracker topper
25. Vertical passage
26. Pledge
27. Blockheads
28. Forebodings
29. Potassium nitrate
30. Group of key personnel
31. Rose
32. Find the answer to
33. Places for important documents
35. Nasal sound
38. Sharp-pointed sword
39. Arabian Sea gulf
40. Least bit
46. Solidify
47. Remove one's boots
48. British measure of capacity
49. One dictated to
50. Dramatic opening
51. Attack
52. Yew or mee
53. Mr. Stravinsky
54. Small bay
55. City in Utah
56. Facts
58. Suffix for baby or boor
59. Unidentified person
61. One who told Moses to speak to Pharaoh

PUZZLE 2

¹S	²H	³E		⁴C	⁵R	⁶A	⁷B		⁸L	⁹O	¹⁰G	¹¹A	¹²N
¹³P	T	A	S		¹⁴H	A	L	E		¹⁵E	R	O	D	E
¹⁶E	R	I	S		¹⁷A	S	T	A		¹⁸S	O	L	I	D
¹⁹W	A	T	E	²⁰R	S	P	O	R	T	S		²²D	T	S
²³S	P	I	N	E	T			²⁴S	E	E	D	S		
			²⁶D	E	C	²⁷A	²⁸A		²⁹A	R	O	M	A	S	³⁰	³¹
³²L	³³A	³⁴D	³⁵D	S		³⁶A	W	³⁷E	S		³⁸M	I	C	E
³⁹O	T	O	E		⁴⁰P	L	A	C	E		⁴¹E	T	R	E
⁴²F	O	U	L		⁴³E	M	I	R		⁴⁴A	S	H	E	N
⁴⁵T	E	N	T	⁴⁶E	D		⁴⁷T	U	⁴⁸R	N				
		⁴⁹G	A	L	A	⁵⁰S			⁵¹U	T	⁵²A	⁵³H	⁵⁴A	⁵⁵N
⁵⁶A	⁵⁷P	R		⁵⁸A	L	P	⁵⁹H	⁶⁰A	B	E	T	I	Z	E
⁶¹L	E	A	⁶²S	T		⁶³R	A	U	L		⁶⁴O	N	U	S
⁶⁵O	L	D	I	E		⁶⁶E	I	R	E		⁶⁷M	Y	R	S
⁶⁸T	E	E	N	S		⁶⁹E	R	A	S		⁷⁰S	S	E	

ACROSS

1. Quarrels
6. Donna or Walter
10. Borders
14. Insertion mark
15. Highest point
16. Operatic melody
17. Priest's place
18. Bulletin board insertion
20. Hovel or palace: abbr.
21. Yellowish substance
23. Actress Adoree
24. __ out a living; got by
25. Guy with a mean brother
27. Wanted badly
30. Ancient Arcadian town
31. Wall and others: abbr.
34. Helping hand
35. End prematurely
36. Prefix for angular or lingual
37. "Are you going to __ ..."
41. Get in the other direction
42. Revise
43. Feed the pot
44. Poet's word
45. *Citizen* __ ; 1941 film
46. Prison employee
48. Quite forward
49. Messenger
50. Coupon user
53. Resentful
54. Boxer
57. Sends
60. Prominent
62. Come to shore
63. Away from the wind
64. Hidden treasure
65. Señor's shouts
66. Persians & Pekingese
67. Brownish shade

DOWN

1. Pockmark
2. Pastel-like
3. Liberal __
4. Cup contents
5. High-cholesterol risk
6. Assessed
7. Canyon sound
8. Kookaburra's neighbor
9. Wilson or Polk: abbr.
10. Fierce badger
11. UN member
12. Mickey and family
13. Word following Pete's
   or heaven's
19. Air taken in and
   then let out
22. Guided
24. At all times
25. Spoken
26. Floe
27. Societal division
28. Holey utensil
29. "Haste makes waste" or
   "A stitch in time saves nine"
30. Have __ to pick;
   take issue
31. Leave one's seat
32. Hackneyed
33. Warning sound
35. Don't exist
38. Cookie makers
39. Bradley
40. Rider's fee
46. Persian Gulf or Civil
47. Proxies
48. Remains unsettled
49. Sits for pix
50. French commune
51. Russian sea
52. Direction indicator
53. Opposite of *dele*
54. Preposition
55. Mr. Strauss
56. Mental image
58. Geography chart
59. Martinique or Miquelon
61. Unprocessed substance

PUZZLE 3

1 S	2 P	3 A	4 T	5 S	■	6 R	7 E	8 E	9 D	■	10 R	11 I	12 M	13 S
14 C	A	R	E	T	■	15 A	C	M	E	■	16 A	R	I	A
17 A	L	T	A	R	■	18 T	H	U	M	19 B	T	A	C	K
20 R	E	S	■	21 O	22 L	E	D	■	■	23 R	E	N	E	E
■	■	■	24 E	K	E	S	■	25 A	26 B	E	L	■	■	■
27 C	28 R	29 A	V	E	D	■	30 A	L	E	A	■	31 S	32 T	33 S
34 A	F	D	E	■	■	35 A	B	O	R	T	■	36 T	R	I
37 S	C	A	R	38 B	39 O	R	O	U	G	H	40 F	A	I	R
41 T	E	G	■	42 A	M	E	N	D	■	■	43 A	N	T	E
44 E	R	E	■	45 K	A	N	E	■	46 W	47 A	R	D	E	N
■	■	■	48 P	E	R	T	■	49 P	A	G	E	■	■	■
50 S	51 A	52 V	E	R	■	■	53 S	O	R	E	■	54 A	55 L	56 I
57 T	R	A	N	S	58 M	59 I	T	S	■	60 N	61 O	T	E	D
62 L	A	N	D	■	63 A	L	E	E	■	64 T	R	O	V	E
65 O	L	E	S	■	66 P	E	T	S	■	67 S	E	P	I	A

ACROSS

1. Oval objects
5. Wall covering
10. PTA member
14. Send
15. Unrestrained
16. Like peas in __
17. Floor piece
18. Río de la __
19. France's Coty
20. One-time baseball VIP
23. Bed-and-breakfast
     establishments
24. Word with every or some
25. Morning aroma
28. Explanatory drawings
33. TV's Kate and __
34. Roger or Demi
35. Roulette risk
36. Political alliance
37. Spherical
38. Lugosi or Bartok
39. Melody
40. Tortilla chip
     accompaniment
41. African badger
42. Like space offered in
     many office buildings
44. Fairly large group
45. Globe
46. Force
47. One-time tennis VIP
54. Bitter substance
55. Small amount
56. Eleanor's nickname
58. Drought-stricken
59. Join
60. Highlander
61. River in Germany
62. Acts
63. Iditarod vehicle

DOWN

1. Suffix for strong or long
2. Followers of a
    failing grade
3. __ monster
4. General's opposite
5. Of a famous range
6. Parts
7. Loud noise
8. Regarding
9. Coastal area
10. Silas of fiction
11. Gorillas' cousins
12. Numerical prefix
13. Seaport in Yemen
21. Part of the leg
22. One who wrote Come
     Back, Little Sheba
25. Political plot
26. Hardy, for short
27. Plants, collectively
28. Do a firefighter's job
29. Island off Scotland
30. Helps to do wrong
31. Noisy conflict
32. Delay
34. Bull's portrayer on
     Night Court
37. Fitted wood joints together
38. Loose temporary stitches
40. Foreign garment
41. Smelly
43. Fuse metals
44. Yearners
46. Went out with
47. Contemptible
48. Decorated with sweet,
     creamy flowers
49. Italian banker's concern
50. Turner's new wife
51. This: Sp.
52. Actress Patricia
53. __ club
57. Atty.'s degree

PUZZLE 4

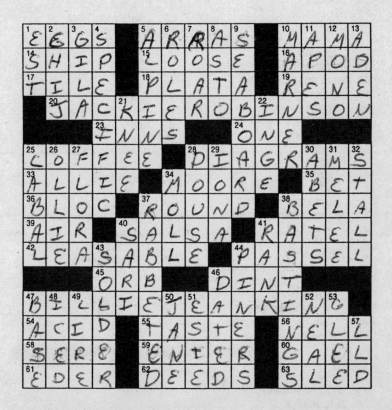

E	E	G	S		A	R	R	A	S		M	A	M	A
S	H	I	P		L	O	O	S	E		A	P	O	D
T	I	L	E		P	L	A	T	A		R	E	N	E
	J	A	C	K	I	E	R	O	B	I	N	S	O	N
		I	N	N	S			O	N	E				
C	O	F	F	E	E		D	I	A	G	R	A	M	S
A	L	L	I	E		M	O	O	R	E		B	E	T
B	L	O	C		R	O	U	N	D		B	E	L	A
A	I	R		S	A	L	S	A		R	A	T	E	L
L	E	A	S	A	B	L	E		P	A	S	S	E	L
			O	R	B			D	I	N	T			
B	I	L	L	I	E	J	E	A	N	K	I	N	G	
A	C	I	D		T	A	S	T	E		N	E	L	L
S	E	R	B		E	N	T	E	R		G	A	E	L
E	D	E	R		D	E	E	D	S		S	L	E	D

ACROSS

1. Tuna container
4. Dry and shriveled
8. UN goal
13. Encourage
14. Stumble
15. Became furious
16. Siamese cry
17. Leave the ground
18. Heart chambers
19. Overly fastidious
22. Common street name
23. Neutered
24. Long period of illness
26. Part of a bicycle
29. Odors
32. Vision
36. Back
38. Let
39. Cruel one
40. Food for the wandering
    Israelites
41. Suffix for confer or prefer
42. Word from 13 Down
43. Nautical direction
44. Autumn flower
45. Ornamental sleeve band
47. Foolish person
49. Mistake
51. Fatal
56. *Diamond __*
58. Gradual increases in
    loudness, musically
61. Actress Verdugo
63. FDR's mom
64. Ms. Murray
65. Fathers
66. 1st name for a daredevil
67. Scottish naturalist John
    (1838-1914)
68. One of the senses
69. __ off; begins a game
70. RR depot: var.

DOWN

1. Move slowly
2. Aristotle's mall?
3. Informative
4. Walk
5. Mr. Sevareid
6. Jeopardy
7. Ensheathed blades
8. Sunday school opener
9. Munch
10. Concord
11. Cover a room with plaster
12. Dutch export
13. Officials
20. Home in a tree
21. Crown
25. Punctures
27. Sea in Russia
28. Belief
30. Suffix for attend
    and accept
31. Brit. currency
32. Living room item
33. Frankenstein's aide
34. Complainers
35. Hi
37. Afresh
40. Alma __
44. Sun disk
46. Cover completely
48. Noble principles
50. Readjust
52. President whose son
    became President
53. Finger food
54. Vladimir Ilyich __
55. River in Europe
56. For fear that
57. Hipbones
59. Fill one's piggy bank
60. Native Canadian
62. Circus safeguard

PUZZLE 5

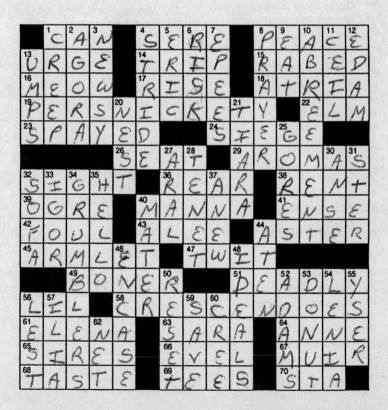

¹C	A	N		⁴S	⁵E	⁶R	⁷E		⁸P	⁹E	A	¹⁰C	¹¹E
¹³U	R	G	E		¹⁴T	R	I	P		¹⁵R	A	B	E	D
¹⁶M	E	O	W		¹⁷R	I	S	E		¹⁸A	T	R	I	A
¹⁹P	E	R	S	²⁰N	I	C	K	E	T	Y		²²E	L	M
²³S	P	A	Y	E	D		²⁴S	I	E	G	²⁵E	
		²⁶S	E	A	²⁷T	²⁸	²⁹A	R	O	M	A	³⁰S	³¹
³²S	³³I	³⁴G	³⁵H	T		³⁶R	E	A	³⁷R		³⁸R	E	N	T
³⁹O	G	R	E		⁴⁰M	A	N	N	A		⁴¹E	N	S	E
⁴²F	O	U	L		⁴³A	L	E	E		⁴⁴A	S	T	E	R
⁴⁵A	R	M	L	⁴⁶E	T		⁴⁷T	W	I	⁴⁸T			
		⁴⁹B	O	N	E	⁵⁰R			⁵¹D	E	⁵²A	⁵³D	⁵⁴L	⁵⁵Y
⁵⁶L	⁵⁷I	L		⁵⁸C	R	E	⁵⁹S	⁶⁰C	E	N	D	O	E	S
⁶¹E	L	E	N	⁶²A		⁶³S	A	R	A		⁶⁴A	N	N	E
⁶⁵S	I	R	E	S		⁶⁶E	V	E	L		⁶⁷M	U	I	R
⁶⁸T	A	S	T	E		⁶⁹T	E	E	S		⁷⁰S	T	A	

ACROSS

1. Ashen
5. Iron or gold
10. Move suddenly
14. Cattleman's item
15. Humiliate
16. Collection of this and that
17. Elec. units
18. From ___; completely
20. "Diamond State": abbr.
21. Convicted ones
22. Author of *The Count of Monte Cristo*
23. Strange twist of circumstances
25. Wee one
26. Elevator alternative
28. Opposite of blesses
31. Change in London
32. Blueprints
34. Portion of land
36. Formerly
37. Like a country bumpkin
38. Expensive painting
39. ___ off; infuriate
40. Find an answer to
41. Rustic shelter
42. Disease-carrying insect
44. Make fun of
45. Spike or Peggy
46. Spay
47. Man the rudder
50. School orgs.
51. Plus
54. ___ stand; hot dog vender's spot
57. Prison: slang
58. Mine entrance
59. Item on a teacher's desk
60. Depend
61. Stewart and others
62. Isle of Man residents
63. Sweetened juices

DOWN

1. Bush, to Yale
2. City built on seven hills
3. Refrigerator and stove
4. Word expressing agreement
5. Bricklayers
6. Heavy wood
7. Letters for Plato
8. Crawling creature
9. Give permission to
10. Policemen's snacks
11. See 1 Down
12. St. ___ of Cascia
13. Fling
19. Fragrances
21. Central part
24. Chicken à la king accompaniment
25. Song
26. Rover's neighbor
27. Doctrine
28. Abode of long, long ago
29. Explained in detail
30. Cylinder or cone, in geometry
32. Anemic
33. IX times VI
35. Minute
37. Feature for Rudolph or Durante
38. Be bold
40. Metric unit
41. Long-running Broadway play
43. Chooses
44. Sky sights
46. Ring-shaped island
47. Skin mark
48. Bustle
49. ___, Oklahoma
50. Word with dream or cleaner
52. Place for gnus and elands to drink
53. Carry Nation & colleagues
55. Rising gas
56. Bath with seats
57. Tortilla maker, often: abbr.

PUZZLE 6

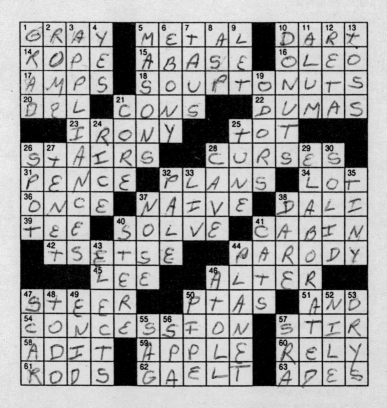

G¹	R²	A³	Y⁴		M⁵	E⁶	T⁷	A⁸	L⁹		D¹⁰	A¹¹	R¹²	T¹³
R¹⁴	O	P	E		A¹⁵	B	A	S	E		O¹⁶	L	E	O
A¹⁷	M	P	S		S¹⁸	O	U	P	T	O¹⁹	N	U	T	S
D²⁰	E	L		C²¹	O	N	S			D²²	U	M	A	S
		I²³	R²⁴	O	N	Y			T²⁵	O	T			
S²⁶	T²⁷	A	I	R	S		C²⁸	U	R	S	E	S²⁹	S³⁰	
P³¹	E	N	C	E		P³²	L³³	A	N	S		L³⁴	O	T³⁵
O³⁶	N	C	E		N³⁷	A	I	V	E		D³⁸	A	L	I
T³⁹	E	E		S⁴⁰	O	L	V	E		C⁴¹	A	B	I	N
	T⁴²	S⁴³	E	T	S	E		P⁴⁴	A	R	O	D	Y	
		L⁴⁵	E	E			A⁴⁶	L	T	E	R			
S⁴⁷	T⁴⁸	E⁴⁹	E	R		P⁵⁰	T	A	S		A⁵¹	N⁵²	D⁵³	
C⁵⁴	O	N	C	E	S⁵⁵	S⁵⁶	I	O	N		S⁵⁷	T	I	R
A⁵⁸	D	I	T		A⁵⁹	P	P	L	E		R⁶⁰	E	L	Y
R⁶¹	O	D	S		G⁶²	A	E	L	T		A⁶³	D	E	S

ACROSS

1. Workplace
4. Not genuine
8. Exclude
13. Pres. Gen. Andres Rodríguez's country
14. See 6 Down
15. Place for a sports event
16. Long-legged bird
17. "When I was __ ..."
18. Lower region
19. Speech given at a toast
22. Canonized lady: abbr.
23. Arm covering
24. Bacon orderer's word
26. Nearly horizontal passage
29. Evergreen tree
32. Virile one
36. Dumbbell
38. Athlete who scored 1281 goals
39. Mr. Knievel
40. Detective's helps
41. At __ ; military command
42. Mythological queen
43. Prefix for gram or space
44. Neatness
45. Prepared
47. Unexpected obstacle
49. One who translates into symbols
51. Curved downward
56. Leader's title
58. Parent, at child's bedtime, often
61. Small mesa
63. River flowing from Belgium
64. Oppose and defy
65. Bass holder
66. Brit. currency
67. __ , Oklahoma
68. Urbanites on a ranch
69. Web-footed bird
70. Born

DOWN

1. Stereotype
2. Leave the ground
3. Tend a roasting turkey
4. Humiliated
5. Headgear for 22 Across
6. With 14 Across, portrayer of the Skipper on *Gilligan's Island*
7. First aid provider
8. Large, showy flower
9. Are flipped
10. Cloth covering
11. Dill herb
12. Level: var.
13. Worst possible condition: slang
20. Name for a Russian boy
21. City in France
25. Gasoline customer's choice
27. Lounging around
28. St. Martin's home
30. "Or __ !"
31. Sidelong look
32. 1965 Beatles movie
33. Word with when or how
34. Like throat lozenges
35. San Antonio site
37. Laborer
40. Academy student
44. Make eyes at
46. Former Ford products
48. Backward
50. Perch
52. Of former times
53. 1896 invention
54. TV's __ , *Indiana*
55. Famous Scott
56. Passing marks
57. Religious teacher
59. Wedding, for one
60. River in France
62. Letter

PUZZLE 7

The completed crossword grid contains the following answers:

Across:
1. LAB
4. SHAM
8. DEBAR
13. PARA
14. HALE
15. ARENA
16. IBIS
17. ALAD
18. HADES
19. TESTIMONIAL
22. STE
23. SLEEVE
24. CRISP
26. ADIT
29. LAUREL
32. HEMAN
36. DOPE
38. PELE
39. EVEL
40. CLUES
41. EASE
42. LEDA
43. AERO
44. ORDER
45. PRIMED
47. SNAG
49. CODER
51. SLOPED
56. AGA
58. STORYTELLER
61. BUTTE
63. OISE
64. DARE
65. CREEL
66. STER
67. ENID
68. DUDES
69. TERN
70. NEE

ACROSS

1. Agreement
5. Colorful liquid
10. Bucks
14. Aroma of flowers
15. Lauder
16. Skin lotion ingredient
17. Road sign
18. Highway patrol setups
20. Help letters
21. Curb
22. Wrong
23. Beloved bishop
25. Croak (less crudely)
26. Job
28. Flag
31. House divisions
32. Friendliness or
    compassion
34. Period
36. Times
37. Hiding places
38. South African fox
39. Time when a train is ex-
    pected to leave: abbr.
40. One who sent the Wise
    Men to find Jesus
41. UCLA athlete
42. Evaluate
44. Unclean
45. Make lace
46. Punitive
47. Despicable person
50. Cause of distress
51. Bank acct.
54. 160-acre parcels, in 1862
57. Completed
58. Ruler's title
59. Burning
60. Subside
61. Word of disgust
62. Endings for some
    girls' names
63. Wraps up

3. "__ of America";
   Indiana's motto
4. Touch lightly
5. Annoy
6. Fluttering tree
7. Object
8. Bess Truman __ Wallace
9. Joe Sr.'s youngest child
10. 1875 Bizet opera
11. Kirghiz's __ Mountains
12. Soaks
13. Notorious German
19. Contaminate
21. Uses one of the senses
24. __ in; surrounds
25. Place for a speaker
26. Canadian tribe member
27. Vital vessel
28. Musical poet
29. Host of a long-running
    variety show
30. Riveter of the '40s
32. Cigarette ingredients
33. Start of Brazil's
    2nd-largest city
35. Take care of
37. In case
38. Song
40. Great amount: colloq.
41. Jaw or hip
43. Controls the direction of
44. Touch and others
46. Man of the cloth
47. Female superstar
48. City in Italia
49. Rising time
50. Worms
52. Rip violently
53. God of war
55. To: Scot.
56. Newt
57. Homonym for a letter

DOWN

1. Decline to bid
2. Means of transportation

PUZZLE 8

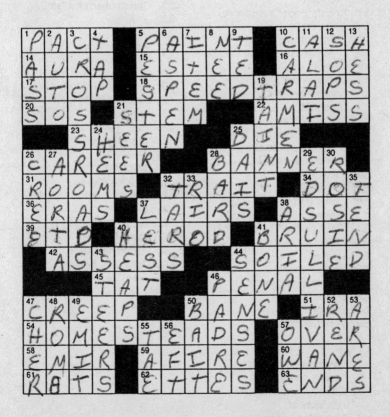

P	A	C	T		P	A	I	N	T		C	A	S	H
A	U	R	A		E	S	T	E	E		A	L	O	E
S	T	O	P		S	P	E	E	D	T	R	A	P	S
S	O	S		S	T	E	M			A	M	I	S	S
		S	H	E	E	N			D	I	E			
C	A	R	E	E	R		B	A	N	N	E	R		
R	O	O	M	S		T	R	A	I	T		D	O	F
E	R	A	S		L	A	I	R	S		A	S	S	E
E	T	D		H	E	R	O	D		B	R	U	I	N
	A	S	S	E	S	S		S	O	I	L	E	D	
		T	A	T			P	E	N	A	L			
C	R	E	E	P		B	A	N	E		I	R	A	
H	O	M	E	S	T	E	A	D	S		O	V	E	R
E	M	I	R		A	F	I	R	E		W	A	N	E
R	A	T	S		E	T	T	E	S		E	N	D	S

ACROSS

1. Hillside
6. Male animal
10. Cutting instrument
14. Unconscious conditions
15. Food made with corn
16. Musical passage
17. Halt, at sea
18. Within: pref.
19. Singing family
20. Snail's feature
22. Change Peking to Beijing
24. Common Latin abbr.
25. Chairpersons' lists
26. Warden
29. Questioning word
30. Pronoun
31. British fencer's weapon
33. Church feature
37. Clumsy transports
39. __ water; do the dog paddle
41. Miffed
42. Like a twang
44. Llamas' home
46. Ingested
47. Crazy people
49. __ down; arranged a place
    for oneself to sleep
51. Smooth dessert
54. Free from sin
55. Relax
56. Ticket that no one wants
60. Home for two
61. Town on the Thames
63. California athlete
64. Uncivil
65. Seldom found
66. Bunker and others
67. Beholds
68. Basks
69. Weather condition

DOWN

1. Opposite of "Welcome!"
2. Strong emotion
3. Country whose capital
   is Muscat
4. Lavender or sky blue
5. Landed properties
6. Short period of time
7. Sound
8. Insect
9. Burns
10. Machines at supermarket
    check-out lines
11. Tent dweller
12. Swelling
13. Lets up
21. Unit of weight
23. Architect Saarinen
25. Leading
26. Rivers
27. Particular atmosphere
28. Sticks in one's craw
29. Christopher and family
32. __ X
34. Urge on
35. Mr. Johnson
36. Have to have
38. Soup accompaniments
40. First appearance
43. Banking transaction
45. Angels
48. Tall __ ; difficult
    assignments
50. Particular
51. Signalers
52. Inappropriate
53. One who spends kronor
54. ▲ ▲ ▲
56. Yellow food
57. Lazy
58. Heraldic bearing
59. Cardinal's home
62. Greek letter

PUZZLE 9

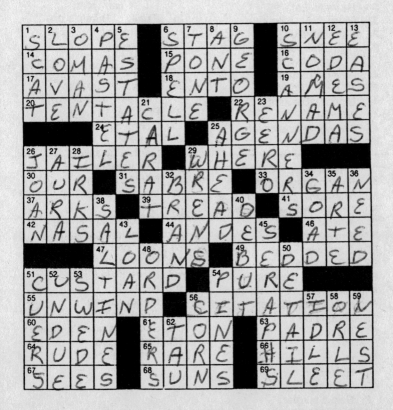

S	L	O	P	E		S	T	A	G		S	N	E	E
C	O	M	A	S		P	O	N	E		C	O	D	A
A	V	A	S	T		E	N	T	O		A	M	E	S
T	E	N	T	A	C	L	E		R	E	N	A	M	E
		E	T	A	L		A	G	E	N	D	A	S	
J	A	I	L	E	R		W	H	E	R	E			
O	U	R		S	A	B	R	E		O	R	G	A	N
A	R	K	S		T	R	E	A	D		S	O	R	E
N	A	S	A	L		A	N	D	E	S		A	T	E
		L	O	O	N	S		B	E	D	D	E	D	
C	U	S	T	A	R	D		P	U	R	E			
U	N	W	I	N	D		C	I	T	A	T	I	O	N
E	D	E	N		E	T	O	N		P	A	D	R	E
R	U	D	E		R	A	R	E		H	I	L	L	S
S	E	E	S		S	U	N	S		S	L	E	E	T

ACROSS

1. Beverage container
6. Room in Acapulco
10. Preposition
14. Electronic servant
15. Not up
16. Fruit holder
17. Sports __
18. Awe
20. Still
21. Ring
23. Spinning
24. Pearl Buck heroine
25. Glove compartment items
27. Series of light, quick taps
30. Prefix for skilled or circle
31. Animal enclosure
34. He was: Lat.
35. Bitter
36. Excessively
37. "__ , all covered
    with snow..."
41. Never, in Nuremberg
42. Think the world of
43. Dinner table item
44. All right
45. Ending for love or for
46. Poplar trees
48. Song subject who "ain't
    what she used to be"
49. French dairy export
50. Traditional peasant's shoe
53. Orange-red piece of jewelry
54. Tumor: suff.
57. Grover
60. County in Texas
62. Italian town
63. Away from the wind
64. Leave out a syllable
65. Iowa's state flower
66. Form of be
67. Places

DOWN

1. Hair color
2. Learning
3. Help a burglar
4. Family member
5. Rice, in China
6. Transparent covering
7. Famous brother
8. Third book: abbr.
9. Beverage
10. Declares formally
11. Utensil part
12. Formerly
13. Part of an apple
19. Section of a river
22. Kernel holder
24. Director Preminger
25. Late actress Oberon
26. Among
27. Showy flower
28. __ Becker;
    L. A. Law role
29. Family of Britain's poet
    laureate (1692-1715)
30. Contempt
31. Shoplifted
32. Symbol
33. Objects that go up
    & down, up & down
35. Prefix for thought
    or mentioned
38. Taste
39. Garlic's giveaway
40. Feel sorry for oneself
46. Departure's opp.
47. Moves in a slow, shy manner
48. Flick
49. Half of a German city?
50. Operation memento
51. Additionally
52. Risky transactions
53. Large knife
54. Neglect
55. Manufactured
56. Greek deity
58. Science student's milieu
59. Foamy liquid
61. Heavyweight

PUZZLE 10

¹G	²L	³A	⁴S	⁵S		⁶S	⁷A	⁸L	⁹A		¹⁰A	¹¹T	¹²O	¹³P
¹⁴R	O	B	O	T		¹⁵A	B	E	D		¹⁶V	I	N	E
¹⁷A	R	E	N	A		¹⁸R	E	V	E	¹⁹R	E	N	C	E
²⁰Y	E	T			²¹P	²²E	A	L			²³A	R	E	E	L
			²⁴O	L	A	N		²⁵M	²⁶A	P	S			
²⁷P	²⁸A	²⁹T	T	E	R		³⁰S	E	M	I		³¹S	³²T	³³Y
³⁴E	R	A	T			³⁵A	C	R	I	D		³⁶T	O	O
³⁷O	N	T	O	P	³⁸O	³⁹F	O	L	D	S	⁴⁰M	O	K	Y
⁴¹N	I	E			⁴²A	D	O	R	E			⁴³O	L	E	O
⁴⁴Y	E	S			⁴⁵L	O	R	N			⁴⁶A	⁴⁷S	P	E	N	S
			⁴⁸M	A	R	E			⁴⁹B	R	I	E		
⁵⁰S	⁵¹A	⁵²B	O	T			⁵³S	A	R	D		⁵⁴O	⁵⁵M	⁵⁶A
⁵⁷C	L	E	V	E	L	A	N	D			⁶⁰L	A	M	A	R
⁶²A	S	T	I			⁶³A	L	E	E			⁶⁴F	L	I	D	E
⁶⁵R	O	S	E			⁶⁶B	E	E	N			⁶⁷S	I	T	E	S

ACROSS

1. Sorrowful cry
5. __ Gras
10. Baby's word
14. __ for; like
15. Anew
16. Lively spirit
17. Row of seats
18. Cheap bars: colloq.
19. Ford product
20. TV personality
23. Nautical term
24. Underhanded one
25. 1st game in a series
28. More like melting snow
33. Staple in Salerno
34. Pick
35. __-pitch softball
36. Egyptian king and
    namesakes
37. Contraction
38. Award given annually
39. Suffix for advert
    or expert
40. White-plumed bird
41. Snow toys
42. Potter
44. Storage area
45. Receive: dial.
46. Black and others
47. "Jessica Fletcher"
54. Midwest export
55. Bulls
56. Forest animals
58. Night in Paris
59. Chili dog topper, for some
60. Greek letters
61. Stops
62. Useful rope
63. Dry

DOWN

1. Skit
2. __ up; disabled
3. Region
4. Maids
5. More furious
6. Nimble
7. Talk deliriously
8. Common New Year's
   resolution
9. Teach
10. Scarcity
11. Grad
12. Facts
13. Shortly
21. Parts of intestines
22. Orient
25. Visual
26. Hesitate
27. Organic compound
28. Partly frozen rain
29. Religious period
30. Man and others
31. Slur over
32. Chanticleer's spot
34. Goes astray
37. Troublemaker
38. Conclusions
40. Late actor Jannings
41. Thick piece
43. Proxies
44. Airplane
46. Nose, humorously
47. Facial problem
48. Part of speech
49. Word with lock or iron
50. Actress Anderson
51. Operatic highlight
52. By __ ; in a routine way
53. Period of time
57. Wind dir.

PUZZLE
11

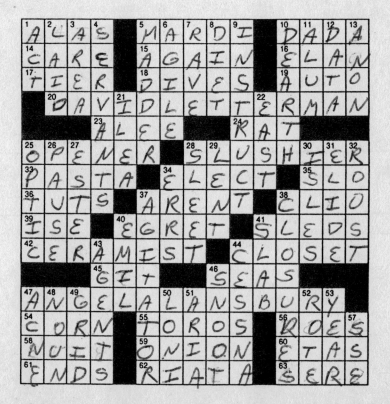

¹A	²L	³A	⁴S		⁵M	⁶A	⁷R	⁸D	⁹I		¹⁰D	¹¹A	¹²D	¹³A
¹⁴C	A	R	E		¹⁵A	G	A	I	N		¹⁶E	L	A	N
¹⁷T	I	E	R		¹⁸D	I	V	E	S		¹⁹A	U	T	O
	²⁰D	A	V	²¹I	D	L	E	T	T	²²E	R	M	A	N
		²³A	L	E	E			²⁴R	A	T				
²⁵O	²⁶P	²⁷E	N	E	R		²⁸S	²⁹L	U	S	H	³⁰I	³¹E	³²R
³³P	A	S	T	A		³⁴E	L	E	C	T		³⁵S	L	O
³⁶T	U	T	S		³⁷A	R	E	N	T		³⁸C	L	I	O
³⁹I	S	E		⁴⁰E	G	R	E	T		⁴¹S	L	E	D	S
⁴²C	E	R	⁴³A	M	I	S	T		⁴⁴C	L	O	S	E	T
			⁴⁵G	I	T		⁴⁶S	E	A	S				
⁴⁷A	⁴⁸N	⁴⁹G	E	L	A	⁵⁰L	A	⁵¹N	S	B	U	R	⁵²Y	⁵³
⁵⁴C	O	R	N		⁵⁵T	O	R	O	S		⁵⁶R	O	E	⁵⁷S
⁵⁸N	U	I	T		⁵⁹O	N	I	O	N		⁶⁰E	T	A	S
⁶¹E	N	D	S		⁶²R	I	A	T	A		⁶³S	E	R	E

ACROSS

1. Lofty range
6. Blotch
10. Westernmost Aleutian island
14. Jeweler's word
15. Use one of the senses
16. Female animals
17. Regal wear
18. Enthrall with sudden love
20. Underhanded
21. Lost a vital fluid
23. Senior
24. Olympic vehicle
25. Weight allowance
27. Musical production
30. Walk about idly
31. Entreat
34. Robert __
35. Bird's place
36. Part of a building
37. Buttons, Betty and Little Boy
41. Work unit
42. Embarrass
43. Famous 1871 opera
44. Snacked
45. Vex
46. Walk like a drunkard
48. Pedestal
49. Word with silver or hard
50. Bits
53. Shopping outlet
54. Small __ ; tots
57. Developed
60. Creative suggestions
62. Pretensions
63. Not here when expected
64. Sudden, sharp increase
65. Printing process, for short
66. Four-legged animal
67. Copy machine additive

DOWN

1. John's follower, in the Good Book
2. Fastener
3. Sturdily built cart
4. Place for a hearing aid
5. Horse's home
6. Recoiled
7. Await decision
8. Clod
9. __-la-la
10. Former minor
11. Amphibian
12. Mitterrand's noggin
13. Addict
19. Swarmed
22. Allow
24. Assassinated
25. Sacred writing
26. Picnic spoiler
27. City in Kentucky
28. Warn
29. Jutting piece
30. Della __
31. Misrepresent
32. Escape
33. Go through bit by bit
35. __ of Two Cities
38. Pester continually
39. Sacred bird of the Nile
40. Naked
46. Detroit export
47. Portrait producer
48. Choir member
49. 39 Down, for one
50. Straight metal beam
51. Hodgepodge
52. Wrongful act
53. Distribute
54. Nonflowering plant
55. Become angry
56. River in Europe
58. Out-of-date
59. West
61. Singing team

PUZZLE 12

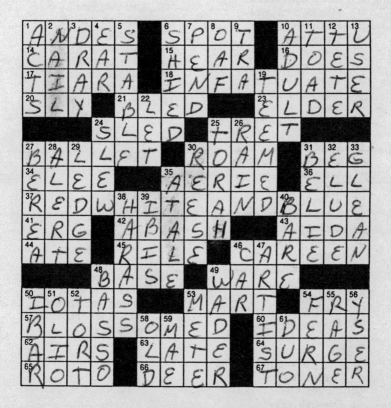

The crossword grid contains the following filled-in answers:

Row 1: ANDES / SPOT / ATTU
Row 2: CARAT / HEAR / DOES
Row 3: TIARA / INFATUATE
Row 4: SLY / BLED / ELDER
Row 5: SLED / TRET
Row 6: BALLET / ROAM / BEG
Row 7: ELEE / AERIE / ELL
Row 8: REDWHITEAND / BLUE
Row 9: ERG / ABASH / AIDA
Row 10: ATE / RILE / CAREEN
Row 11: BASE / WARE
Row 12: IOTAS / MART / FRY
Row 13: BLOSSOMED / IDEAS
Row 14: AIRS / LATE / SURGE
Row 15: ROTO / DEER / TONER

ACROSS

1. Singer's range
5. Tarry
10. Bettor's concern
14. One of two twelves
15. Obliterate
16. __ song; cheaply
17. Names
18. Privilege of the first to
    reach a four-way stop
20. From __ Z
21. Traditional gifts for dad
22. Lets
23. FDR and JFK, to Harvard
25. Jolt
26. Feast
28. Soothing resin
31. Hot under the collar
32. Monroe's follower
34. Five cees
36. Weaponry
37. Wrong
38. Govt. employee
39. Jungle creature
40. Kicking's partner, in phrase
41. Dim
42. Drew on a transparent sheet
44. Pops
45. Three in Tivoli
46. Shows great emotion
47. Use a pan
50. Foreign coin
51. Adherent: suff.
54. Ideas one can't get rid of
57. Orchestra instrument
58. Lands off the
    coast of France
59. Fine personal quality
60. __ mater
61. For fear that
62. Newspapers & magazines
63. Smell

DOWN

1. "... __ partridge in a
   pear tree."
2. Clumsy one
3. Downhill glider
4. Switch positions
5. Make fun of
6. American Indians
7. Fails to keep up
8. __ Wednesday
9. Nevertheless
10. Bids
11. Depressed
12. Phooey!
13. States
19. Examinations
21. Story
24. Rising star
25. Bread spreads
26. Latvian capital
27. Throw forth lava
28. 1st, 2nd or 3rd
29. Like evidence
    allowed in court
30. Intended
32. Hemmed in by
33. Math. procedure
35. Suffixes for respond
    and depend
37. Toward shelter
38. Infield protector,
    during a rainstorm
40. TV's *Green* __
41. Coal or gas
43. Certify by oath
44. Monsters
46. Ports
47. Earth
48. Competent
49. Purposes
50. American Beauty
52. Partial amount
53. Furniture wood
55. Undermine
56. Country est. in 1948
57. Word whose homonym
    has no *a*

PUZZLE 13

¹A	²L	³T	⁴O		⁵D	⁶E	⁷L	⁸A	⁹Y		¹⁰O	¹¹D	¹²D	¹³S
¹⁴M	O	O	N		¹⁵E	R	A	S	E		¹⁶F	O	R	A
¹⁷D	U	B	S		¹⁸R	I	G	H	T	¹⁹O	F	W	A	Y
²⁰A	T	O		²¹T	I	E	S			²²R	E	N	T	S
		²³G	²⁴R	A	D	S			²⁵J	A	R			
²⁶R	²⁷E	G	A	L	E		²⁸B	A	L	S	A	²⁹M	³⁰M	
³¹I	R	A	T	E		³²A	D	A	M	S		³⁴D	E	³⁵E
³⁶G	U	N	S		³⁷A	M	I	S	S		³⁸T	M	A	N
³⁹A	P	E		⁴⁰A	L	I	V	E		⁴¹F	A	I	N	T
	⁴²T	R	⁴³A	C	E	D			⁴⁴B	U	R	S	T	S
		⁴⁵T	R	E			⁴⁶W	E	E	P	S			
⁴⁷S	⁴⁸A	⁴⁹U	T	E		⁵⁰R	I	A	L		⁵¹I	⁵²S	⁵³T	
⁵⁴O	B	S	E	S	⁵⁵S	⁵⁶I	O	N	S		⁵⁷O	B	O	E
⁵⁸I	L	E	S		⁵⁹A	S	S	E	T		⁶⁰A	L	M	A
⁶¹L	E	S	T		⁶²P	R	E	S	S		⁶³R	E	E	R

ACROSS

1. Part of South
    America's coast
6. Otherwise
10. Make a mess
14. Printer's mark
15. Secular
16. Word with dead or head
17. Señorita's confidante
18. Self-confidence
20. Timetable abbr.
21. Los dos, in the U. S.
23. Opposite of exit
24. Medieval, spelled
    medievally
25. Float
27. Pressed a typewriter's bar
30. Company emblem
31. Storage container
34. Meaty concoction
35. Not smashed
36. __ of Good Feeling
    (1817-25)
37. "The Iron Chancellor"
41. V
42. Foreigner
43. Dagger
44. Make a boo-boo
45. Frees
46. Breaks a traffic law
48. African plant
49. Prefix for phrase or legal
50. Upright stone slab
53. Showing good judgment
54. Filled one's tummy
57. Parts of a very formal attire
60. Doomed
62. Handle: Lat.
63. Flutter
64. Antelope
65. Beverage
66. Cincinnati __
67. Deceitful: slang

DOWN

1. Type of school: abbr.
2. Item on a dog tag
3. Boring companion
4. Diagnostic test, for short
5. Unchanging
6. Fill with joy
7. Whip
8. Abby, to Ann
9. Old French coin
10. Inclination
11. Dryer residue
12. Tale opener
13. Nobleman
19. Turn over a new leaf
22. Eccentric
24. Eight: Sp.
25. Sign of spring
26. Grows gray
27. Push
28. Dad, humorously
29. Garden bloom
30. Earring spots
31. Author of *Around the
    World in Eighty Days*
32. Formed a curve
33. Grabs
35. Like a derisive remark
38. Knight's page
39. Mixture of this & that
40. Bewildered
46. Droop
47. Like better
48. Cathedral feature
49. Histories
50. Striker's opposite
51. Sound
52. Comfort
53. Moved smoothly
54. Rat-__
55. Nomad's home
56. Nelson
58. Continent: abbr.
59. __ du Diable
61. Jim Nabors' state
    of birth: abbr.

PUZZLE 14

A	N	D	E	S		E	L	S	E		S	L	O	P
C	A	R	E	T		L	A	I	C		L	I	N	E
A	M	I	G	A		A	S	S	U	R	A	N	C	E
D	E	A		B	A	T	H			E	N	T	E	R
			O	L	D	E		R	A	F	T			
S	P	A	C	E	D		L	O	G	O		V	A	T
H	A	S	H			S	O	B	E	R		E	R	A
O	T	T	O	V	O	N	B	I	S	M	A	R	C	K
V	E	E		A	L	I	E	N			S	N	E	E
E	R	R		R	I	D	S		S	P	E	E	D	S
			A	L	O	E		P	A	R	A			
S	T	E	L	E		G	A	G	E		A	T	E	
C	O	A	T	T	A	I	L	S		F	A	T	E	D
A	N	S	A		F	L	I	T		E	L	A	N	D
B	E	E	R		O	H	I	O		R	A	T	T	Y

ACROSS

1. Leaping ~~amphibian~~
5. ~~Old~~
10. ~~Part sometimes pierced~~
14. Lowdown
15. Fill with pride
16. 37 Across' feature
17. Overdue
18. Law
20. Traveler's dir.
21. Untainted
22. Candy dish items
23. Party honoring a star
25. Atlantic resort, for short
26. Go round and round
28. Very attractive thing
31. Semiprecious stone
32. __ acid
34. Truck
36. Lack of order
37. Bushy-tailed animal
38. Half of a late comedy pair
39. Put up in rollers
40. Soft mud
41. Pop
42. Mariners
44. Extents
45. Down
46. Runner
47. Means of ascent
50. Nemesis
51. One known for raising Cain
54. Fortifying
57. Not imaginary
58. Weather forecast
59. Douse
60. Indigo dye
61. Picnic intruders
62. Abacus
63. One in servitude

DOWN

1. Rectangular piece
2. __ even keel
3. Lingering sensation
4. John __
5. Read
6. Open-eyed
7. Cooking herb
8. Nickname that sounds like a dinner
9. Japanese delicacy
10. ~~Skin softener~~
11. Norse god
12. Italy's shape
19. Chihuahua friend
21. Spread
24. Stable meal
25. Smelly
26. West Coast team
27. Curved moldings
28. Selfish child's word
29. Forest sights
30. Cup: Fr.
32. Related
33. Short flower?
35. Lice
37. Toboggan
38. __ buggy
40. Like a 4.0 student
41. Work with hay
43. Over 50% of the world's people
44. Dead __
46. Home near a church
47. Poison remedies
48. Civil service agent, for short
49. Just __ ; somewhat
50. Tie
52. In __ ; irreverently
53. That madame
55. "The flowers that bloom in the spring, __ ..."
56. Top
57. Actress Charlotte

¹F	²r	³o	⁴g		⁵y	⁶o	⁷u	⁸n	⁹g		¹⁰B	¹¹o	¹²B	¹³e
¹⁴					¹⁵						¹⁶O			
¹⁷					¹⁸					¹⁹	t			
²⁰				²¹						²²	i			
		²³	²⁴						²⁵		o			
²⁶	²⁷							²⁸			n		²⁹	³⁰
³¹					³²	³³						³⁴		³⁵
³⁶				³⁷							³⁸			
³⁹				⁴⁰					⁴¹					
	⁴²		⁴³					⁴⁴						
		⁴⁵					⁴⁶							
⁴⁷	⁴⁸	⁴⁹				⁵⁰					⁵¹	⁵²	⁵³	
⁵⁴				⁵⁵	⁵⁶					⁵⁷				
⁵⁸				⁵⁹						⁶⁰				
⁶¹				⁶²						⁶³				

ACROSS

1. Male animal
6. Become larger
10. Store away
14. Shiraz resident
15. Assess
16. Big book
17. Summarize
18. Comes before
20. Afr. nation
21. Cup + cup
23. Deputy
24. Winter Olympics vehicle
25. Word with Pete's or gosh
27. Calling
30. Besides
31. Rejuvenating spring
34. Father of a famous pair
35. Work with hair
36. Color
37. Be self-evident
41. Poet's word
42. Dens
43. Last of the Stuart
    monarchs
44. German article
45. Wings
46. One who signs illegally
48. Howls
49. Musical group
50. Medal
53. Spiritual slip-ups
54. Stupid person
57. Destroy
60. Public proclamation
62. Item for Palmer
63. Smell
64. Now
65. Look after
66. Cleans the floor
67. Look steadily

DOWN

1. Regal address
2. Allowance fixed
    by weight
3. __ other; one another
4. Last queen of Spain
5. Small wave
6. Word with jury or piano
7. Carry on
8. Mel the Giant
9. Itsy-bitsy
10. Level of development
11. Carryall
12. Sign
13. Go-young man connector
19. Word with North or South
22. Suffix for crunch or grouch
24. Truck
25. Pieces of wood
26. Without any changes
27. Like a zoo animal
28. Glorify
29. Less refined
30. Astringents
31. Smart
32. Lustrous cloth
33. Hothead's problem
35. Combines
38. Tire features
39. Word with Thursday
    or Toledo
40. Measurement
46. Aficionado
47. Beginnings
48. Cattle mark
49. Coffin platforms
50. Entry to a mine
51. Common verb
52. Cosmetic producer
53. Cease
54. Verdi production
55. Reminder of a
    past operation
56. Small swelling
58. Cruise
59. Bother
61. Speck

1	2	3	4	5		6	7	8	9		10	11	12	13
14						15					16			
17						18			19					
20				21	22					23				
			24					25	26					
27	28	29					30					31	32	33
34					35						36			
37			38	39						40				
41			42						43					
44			45					46	47					
		48					49							
50	51	52				53					54	55	56	
57				58	59				60	61				
62				63				64						
65				66				67						

ACROSS

1. Exchange
5. Sweet treats
10. Bag
14. Centennial State: abbr.
15. Of a region
16. Govt. agent
17. Tax-deferred accts.
18. Post Office counter item
19. __ , Nevada
20. Place to store dishes
23. University student
24. __ code
25. Sandal parts
28. Address to a cardinal
33. Not all __ ; nutty
34. Arctic Ocean sights
35. Exclamations
36. Attack
37. Violet or rose
38. Design
39. Name with Jo or Mary
40. Jennifer or James Earl
41. Heavy weight lifter
42. Falls
44. Eastwood and others
45. __ out; release
46. Injure
47. Donut-shaped objects
54. Site of the Natl.
    Cowboy Hall of Fame
55. Coeur d'__ , Idaho
56. Despicable
58. Hamburger
59. Elegance
60. President Arthur's
    middle name
61. Invites
62. Adieux
63. Parts of a journey

DOWN

1. __-fi
2. Daily grind
3. Jai __
4. Piece of mail
5. Crushes
6. Curved
7. Gaunt
8. Powder ingredient
9. Shabbier
10. Flag's symbol for
    each colony
11. So it is!
12. Bamboo stem
13. Shoelace problem
21. Deal with problems
22. Flour containers
25. Expensive instrument,
    for short
26. Scottish clan chief
27. Means of control
28. Those French women
29. Pasture sounds
30. Baseball's Ryan
31. Intone
32. Domestics of old
34. __ of; having a liking for
37. Written agreement
38. Of the earliest times
40. GI's transport
41. II x VII x XI
43. Track shoe features
44. Show affection for
46. High-IQ group
47. Small hill: Sp.
48. Men for Mamie and Tina
    (once)
49. Strong opposition
50. Ms. Fitzgerald
51. Chair
52. Anger
53. Smelting refuse
57. __ , Os, ...

PUZZLE 17

ACROSS

1. TV show of the '80s
6. Smack
10. "__ she blows!"
14. Support
15. Item made of rubber
16. Bylaw
17. __ Rica
18. Instructed once again
20. Color
21. Obedient
23. Pens
24. Cry for assistance
25. Nome transport
27. Give confidence to
30. Black substance
31. Boo-hoo
34. Furl
35. Opposite of excitement
36. Full deck
37. Kid's kid's kid
41. Western Indian
42. Manilow
43. __ fixe
44. Special sense
45. Oklahoma native
46. Backward
48. Nonpareil
49. Incisions
50. Want very much
53. Runner
54. L. A. __
57. Settle on unoccupied land
60. Get rid of
62. State
63. Do a lawn chore
64. Like school paper
65. __ up; confined
66. Eccentric old fellow
67. Counter orders

DOWN

1. Passing grades
2. Donahue
3. Alleviate
4. Performance
5. Scanty
6. Razor sharpener
7. Was deceitful
8. College major
9. Word with cent or chance
10. Threesome
11. Like some juries
12. Nautical direction
13. 1981 Oscar winning film
19. Containing vinegar
22. Bullfight sound
24. Graceful dance
25. Father of Chastity
26. Boisterous
27. Dispute
28. Varieties
29. Slumber
30. Trap
31. Piece of playground equipment
32. Texas athlete
33. Senator from Delaware
35. Oversight
38. Steaks
39. Entryway
40. Singles, doubles, et al.
46. Part of the summer: abbr.
47. Toughens
48. Apparent
49. Trainee
50. Man
51. Wander
52. Word expressing agreement
53. Half of a Samoan seaport?
54. Ground
55. On the waves
56. Joins
58. Investigator, for short
59. Taro root
61. Coastal resort, familiarly

	1	2	3	4	5			6	7	8	9			10	11	12	13
14							15						16				
17							18					19					
20					21	22						23					
			24						25	26							
27	28	29						30						31	32	33	
34						35							36				
37				38	39							40					
41				42								43					
44				45						46	47						
			48						49								
50	51	52					53						54	55	56		
57					58	59					60	61					
62					63						64						
65					66						67						

ACROSS

1. Uninteresting
5. Recommendation for
   sore muscles
8. Astonishes
12. Islands off Timor
13. Latin American dance
16. Be
17. __ about; circa
18. Decree
19. Mental image
20. Arrive at an agreement
23. Do wrong
24. Roosted
25. Pleasant looks
27. Weaken
30. Word with nut or cock
32. Turtle
35. Cross
38. Brought
39. River flowing from Belgium
40. Full
43. Transfer ownership of
44. Pretty bloom
46. Restore a motor
48. Simple shelters: var.
51. Lawyers' org.
52. Start of a U. S. capital
53. Utilizations
55. Santa __ , California
57. Wide's companion,
    in phrase
59. Acting out
64. End in __ ;
    come out even
66. Musical number
67. __ Mountains
68. Sleep
69. Carrier
70. Uncommon
71. Type of sword
72. Hissing sound
73. Suffix for persist or infer

DOWN

1. Word whose homonym
   ends with *k*
2. TV's Jay
3. __ bomb
4. Employs
5. Children's vehicles
6. Norfolk, Seattle or Boston
7. Coastal mountains
8. Ring champ
9. Very extensive
10. Word with green
    or lasting
11. Scorch
14. Disease causers
15. __ arm; very
    close together
21. Present wrapper's item
22. Thick piece
26. Historical period
27. Small wild mammal
28. Get out of bed
29. Process milk
31. White __ sheet
33. Endow with talents
34. Spools
36. Humphrey & Rockefeller
37. WWII area
41. *Uncle Tom's Cabin*
    character
42. Arguers
45. Peruse
47. Member of royalty
49. Wading bird
50. Former intl. alliance
54. Marks with sooty matter
56. Blue
57. Become dim
58. Preposition
60. Kids' refreshments
61. Mideast nation
62. Drugbuster
63. Delight
65. Sneaker letters

PUZZLE 19

ACROSS

1. Calculate
4. Florida seaport
9. Laborious
13. Fruit
15. Local expression
16. Busy as __
17. Subdue
18. Dawn
19. Playing card
20. Make laws
22. Quit
23. Beat badly
24. Old car
26. Cross out
29. Speaks with difficulty
34. Ms. Hill, of the Clarence Thomas controversy
35. Encircle a fort
36. Large container
37. Casks
38. Dessert
39. Ms. Moreno
40. Poet's word
41. Thick soup
42. Understood
43. Jagged
45. Duplicates
46. __ on Melancholy
47. Breathe heavily
48. Kilted one
51. In a sideways direction
56. Festive dance
57. Deputy
58. __ Indies
60. Rat's follower
61. Divine influence
62. Was sorry about
63. Remove
64. Relaxed
65. Kildare and Casey: abbr.

DOWN

1. Attached res.
2. Good buy
3. British title
4. Crier's need
5. Mature
6. 100 drachmas, in old Egypt
7. Stick one's lower lip out
8. Electrical current's strength
9. Good-looking 19th-century carriage?
10. Just __ ; somewhat
11. City northeast of Lake Tahoe
12. Word with South or freeze
14. Send one's __ ; decline an invitation
21. Jot
25. Uncle who wears a kilt
26. Social activities
27. Harden
28. Ocean sight
29. Was a father to
30. Mere's head
31. Force out
32. Proportion
33. Numerical info
35. Angry
38. Instruction
39. Reptile
41. Launch site
42. Actress Louise
44. Turn
45. Left suddenly
47. Change for Oliver Twist
48. Coastal fish
49. Sheep shelter
50. Roberts
52. City in India
53. Refreshments served hot or cold
54. Praise
55. River in Europe
59. Cowboys' goals: abbr.

1	2	3			4	5	6	7	8		9	10	11	12
13			14		15						16			
17					18						19			
	20			21							22			
		23						24	25					
26	27	28					29	30				31	32	33
34						35						36		
37					38						39			
40				41						42				
43			44						45					
			46					47						
48	49	50			51	52	53					54	55	
56					57						58			59
60					61						62			
63					64						65			

ACROSS

1. Splendor
5. Org. for neurologists & oncologists
8. Part of a staircase
12. Billy Joel's nationality: abbr.
13. Measures the circumference of
16. Son of a folk singer
17. Agcy. founded by DDE in 1958
18. Panel sewn into a garment
19. Unhealthy looking
20. Opposite of modern
23. Ping-Pong table's centerpiece
24. Harem room
25. Books
27. Black cuckoo
30. Suffix denoting origin
32. Backs out of an agreement
35. Showing no intelligence
38. Transparent wrap
39. Lowdown
40. Engraved pillar: var.
43. 100 centavos
44. Weather forecast
46. One who produces formal wedding invitations
48. Runts
51. Present
52. Way to go: abbr.
53. Cloth named for a city
55. Feminine one: Sp.
57. Co. that merged with GE in 1986
59. Paid
64. Highly spiced stew
66. Common verb
67. Shine's partner, in phrase
68. Pick over
69. Scoop
70. Saudi Arabia's neighbor
71. Openers
72. Melancholy
73. Like a spayed animal: abbr.

DOWN

1. Appear to be out of breath
2. Sharif
3. Tableland
4. Spain's national museum
5. Stirs up
6. Prefix for bus or bike
7. Criminal offense
8. Pinhead
9. Sin
10. French pronoun
11. Shakespeare, for one
14. Pavarotti or Caruso
15. Barrel piece
21. Singer Billy
22. Part of the eye
26. Jumps
27. Askew
28. Final part of a baseball game, usually
29. Casually
31. Suffix for mild or wild
33. Abates
34. Nasal sound
36. Ill-fated Andrea __
37. 5th word of *The Star-Spangled Banner*
41. Connected letters
42. Teemed
45. DCL quadrupled
47. Has
49. Roam about furtively
50. Pacific island group
54. Idaho exports
56. 1st entry in *Names for Boys*
57. Hudson, for one
58. Hint
60. __ Fitzgerald
61. "At the tone, the __ will be..."
62. Famous twin
63. Car blemish
65. Pacino and Unser

ACROSS
1. Jeer
6. __ with; tolerate
10. Part of a ticket
14. Beverage
15. Said aloud
16. El __
17. Change
18. Made legally binding
20. Famous Chairman
21. Way of conducting oneself
23. Clear the slate
24. Group of animals
25. See 19 Down
27. Warning sign
30. Earring's place
31. Eur. language
34. Skating rink
35. Domesticates
36. Sticky stuff
37. Outwits
41. Suffix for depart or script
42. Like a juicier peach
43. Gambler's mecca
44. Isr.'s neighbor
45. Seed covering
46. Bowl-shaped cavity
48. __ tea
49. Mouse's feature
50. Get away from
53. Overlaid with gold
54. Reverence
57. Stuntman
60. Stomach problem
62. Canadian prov.
63. Shopper's delight
64. Marksman
65. Hodgepodge
66. Organizers of school
    carnivals: abbr.
67. City in England

DOWN
1. Pigeon's pitfall
2. Vending machine purchase
3. Numerical prefix
4. Unfriendly one
5. Dell resident
6. Cherished
7. Shiraz's locale
8. Harper, for short
9. Samuel's teacher
10. Bowling term
11. "See ya!"
12. Takes advantage of
13. Foretell
19. Abhor
22. Dander
24. Linden and others
25. Best of all hits
26. "Wanna make __ ?"
27. Counterfeit
28. Word with one or day
29. 74% of the earth's surface
30. Stereotype
31. Long-legged bird
32. Not you, or me,
    or anybody else
33. "__ it!"; words of
    encouragement
35. Lacking enthusiasm
38. Drew over
39. Take on
40. Of an epoch
46. Presidential nickname
47. Ceremony
48. Opinions
49. Floor pieces
50. Cheese-exporting town
51. Stretch of lowland
52. Ballet and ceramics
53. __ monster
54. Top
55. Unwanted growth
56. Misjudges
58. Intuitive power
59. Tub
61. Recline

PUZZLE 22

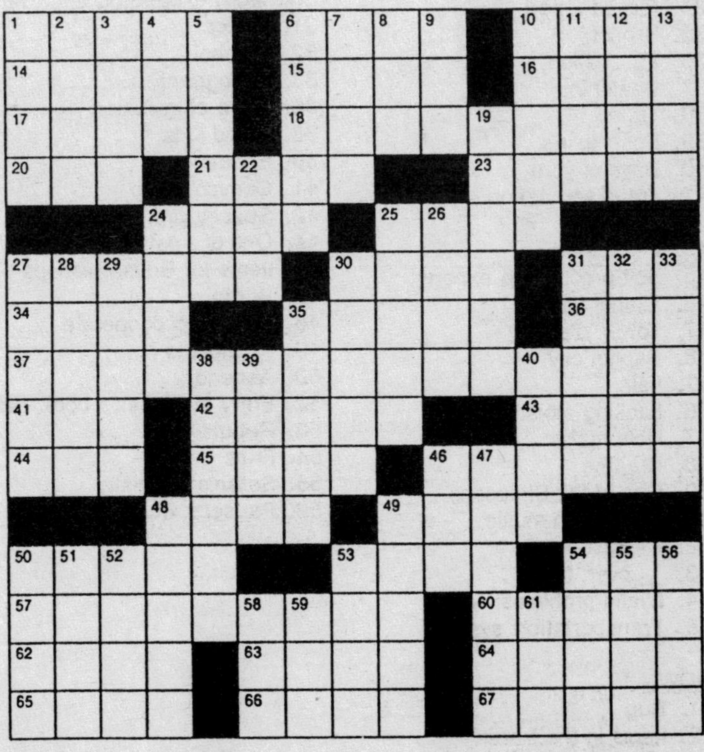

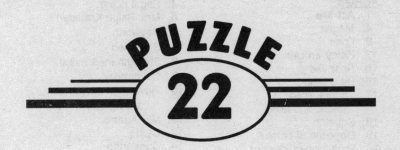

ACROSS

1. Act like
4. Magna __
9. Over
13. Holey articles
15. Roar like __
16. Hard lump
17. Tortilla--fried, folded and filled
18. Squelch
19. Opposite of comin'
20. Fruit-topped dessert
22. Persons
23. Prefix for marketing or communication
24. Egypt's loc.
26. Giggle
29. Ships' stabilizers
34. Played a part
35. Brooch
36. Eur. nation
37. Deafening
38. Trifled
39. Resembling
40. Days of yore
41. Fraus and señoras
42. Famous
43. Fluctuated
45. Self-proclaimed experts
46. Timber tree
47. Tower site
48. Capital city
51. Fair
56. Lacking moisture
57. Hole-maker
58. Breathe
60. One of the Simpsons
61. Sweetly, in music
62. Mideast bigwig
63. __ over; faint
64. Eyelid problems: var.
65. Transportation systems

DOWN

1. Bug
2. Items in the frozen food section
3. Impress sharply
4. Regal home
5. Mrs. Ralph Kramden
6. Hayworth
7. Snatched
8. Strengthened metal
9. Cat or goat
10. Time when the hands are together
11. Ms. Adams
12. Cysts
14. Comforted
21. Marsh growth
25. Eb's wife, in comics
26. Narratives
27. Sorbonne, for one
28. Practice piece
29. Howled
30. Word expressing approval
31. Malice
32. Symbol
33. Toboggans
35. Word of invitation
38. Blond kids
39. Endearing
41. Common verb
42. Spacey org.?
44. One of a pair
45. Items for British bishops
47. Portion
48. Refuse to cooperate
49. __ Indians
50. Ascend
52. Entry in Bartlett's book: abbr.
53. Repulsive
54. Fruit
55. Satan's specialty
59. Pauser's words

PUZZLE
23

1	2	3			4	5	6	7	8		9	10	11	12
13			14		15						16			
17					18						19			
	20			21							22			
		23							24	25				
26	27	28					29	30				31	32	33
34						35						36		
37					38						39			
40				41						42				
43			44						45					
			46				47							
48	49	50			51	52	53					54	55	
56					57					58				59
60					61					62				
63					64						65			

ACROSS

1. Word of lament
5. Human trunks
10. Location
14. Wait
15. Of erns & terns
16. What __ you; anything else of a similar sort
17. Handicapped
18. Capital city
20. Assam silkworm
21. Sporting equipment
22. Occasion
23. Bawl out
25. Exist
26. Take for granted
28. Blustery conditions
31. Ending for York or Worcester
32. Miles per hour
34. Ripe old age
36. One of Hamlet's choices
37. Scrub
38. D doubled plus 151
39. Bird with a sharp sense of sight and sound
40. City in New York
41. Color
42. Cowardly
44. Dwells on with delight
45. __ to; increase
46. Soupy
47. Without __ ; happy-go-lucky
50. Items on a list to Santa
51. Barracks feature
54. In a marvelous way
57. Region
58. Narrow way
59. Long for
60. King Kong and family
61. Brit. currency
62. Becomes bored
63. Bother

DOWN

1. Qualified
2. One not to be trusted
3. Like some court evidence
4. Use one of the senses
5. Football position
6. Egg-shaped
7. __ off; robs
8. So, on the braes
9. Place to spend the night
10. Lad: colloq.
11. Part of a book
12. Hot spot
13. Item made of canvas
19. John the Baptist's imprisoner
21. Indefinite amount
24. Remedy
25. Sun disk
26. In the matter of
27. Ostentatious
28. Connery or Penn
29. Lab item
30. __ system
32. Committed homicide
33. Tiny, round item
35. Paintings
37. Clumsy one
38. Relocate
40. More mature
41. 30th president & others
43. Place where food is kept
44. Give permission
46. Find the answer to
47. Leather workers' tools
48. Garment
49. Ms. Bancroft
50. Title for former rulers
52. Bills
53. Trial
55. All Saints' Day's forerunner: abbr.
56. Swiss canton
57. Hit with a stun gun

PUZZLE
24

1	2	3	4		5	6	7	8	9		10	11	12	13
14					15						16			
17					18					19				
20				21						22				
		23	24						25					
26	27						28				29	30		
31					32	33					34		35	
36					37					38				
39				40					41					
	42		43					44						
		45					46							
47	48	49				50					51	52	53	
54				55	56					57				
58				59						60				
61				62						63				

ACROSS

1. Tokyo accessory
4. Parts of a horse's collar
9. Boast
13. Unit of force
15. Stay
16. Term of affection
17. Home for over half of
    the people in the world
18. Less mannerly
19. Verily
20. Leaping about
22. Monthly expense
23. Sponsorship
24. Bleating animal
26. Stands in awe of
29. General Arnold and others
34. Author of *The Red
    Badge of Courage*
35. Bringing civil action against
36. Nonsense
37. Warehouse pests
38. Mechanical device
39. Opposite of 12 Down
40. __ out; supplement
41. Part of a Girl Scout uniform
42. Better
43. Church events
45. City in Ohio
46. Recent tyrant
47. Orange-red jewelry
48. Piece of paper
51. Enticing one
56. Serve chowder
57. Of orioles and owls
58. Baptism or wedding
60. Bakery worker
61. Blair or Hunt
62. Iditarod vehicle
63. G.I.'s dinner
64. Shut-eye
65. Cries of pain

DOWN

1. Eggs: Lat.
2. Fruit variety
3. Hip portions
4. Brer Rabbit's creator
5. Touches
6. Part of France
7. Garden spot
8. Corporal's superior
9. Wine
10. St. Peter's burial place
11. Cake's spot, for an
    hour or so
12. Left
14. Bars
21. Type of arch
25. Head covering
26. Land units
27. Duck's partner
28. Western
29. TVs: colloq.
30. Police problem
31. Praying figure
32. Star-crossed lover
33. Ship's end
35. Painful
38. Musical programs
39. Ashes
41. Bridge term
42. Corporal Max Klinger
44. Reptiles
45. XL winks
47. One of 13 in 52
48. Slender
49. Add a little rum to the punch
50. Bad day for Julius
52. Vile
53. Selfish child's word
54. Storage building
55. Worry
59. Bradley and Koch

ACROSS

1. Grumpy person
5. Out of one's mind
8. Villain
12. Prefix for dialysis or globin
13. Deep pit, to a poet
16. Cartoon caveman
17. Brainchild
18. Caroline, to Ted
19. Melody
20. Thoughtful
23. Franklin, to friends
24. Refrain syllable
25. Pieces of asparagus
27. Men's nicknames
30. Letter for Plato
32. Elaborate residences
35. Like ancient Rome,
    at the time of its Fall
38. Wooden slat
39. Shape
40. Hurts one's toe
43. Increased
44. President whose hus-
    band was a president
46. Frostbite complication
48. Youths: slang
51. "Croak"
52. Former div. of a large nation
53. Lucky Charms
55. Container for 7 Down
57. Taxing time: abbr.
59. Considered carefully
64. One of a pair
66. Flat
67. Prefix for graph or trooper
68. Imitates a cow
69. Strike
70. Mideast prince
71. Otherwise
72. Family tree member
73. Smell

DOWN

1. Fashionable
2. Complete again
3. TV comedy
4. Toot one's own horn
5. Orders
6. Rose's lover, in story
7. Color changers
8. Many times, to a poet
9. Monies advanced
   to a prospector
10. Common name on
    the Left Bank
11. Genesis setting
14. Suffix for sea or land
15. __ out; distributes
21. Rankled
22. Food: colloq.
26. Assessor
27. Take into the family
28. River bank
29. Oz visitor, and others
31. Insect
33. Makes smooth
34. 4/18/92 meal
36. Isolated
37. Pull
41. Disobedient
42. Complained in a
    whining, tearful way
45. Weirdo
47. __ up; increase efficiency
49. Feels dizzy
50. Capital city
54. Pale
56. Become less and less
57. Word that means the
    same when *cap* is
    added to the front
58. Popular backyard feature
60. Second in a series
61. Submissive
62. __ Indians
63. Like the night
65. Part of Mao's name

1	2	3	4		5	6	7				8	9	10	11
12					13			14	15		16			
17					18						19			
20				21						22		23		
			24				25				26			
27	28	29		30		31		32					33	34
35			36				37			38				
39					40			41	42		43			
44				45			46			47				
48					49	50		51				52		
		53					54		55		56			
57	58			59				60				61	62	63
64			65		66						67			
68					69						70			
71						72					73			

ACROSS

1. __ - CIO
4. Family of a German philosopher
9. Unhealthy sound
13. Lingerie shop purchase
15. Intestinal part
16. Malicious
17. Fruit with a distinctive shape
18. Dance for the agile
19. Bill
20. Mr. Right
22. Babe's place
23. Ein + zwei
24. Chapeau
26. Fix
29. Christmas purchases
34. Ms. Bryant
35. Approaches
36. Cry of discovery
37. Completed
38. Out of __
39. __ to; like
40. Potable
41. Peaks
42. *Goodnight,* __
43. Impetuosity
45. Base stealer, often
46. Midi summer
47. Fives
48. Like a skyscraper
51. Letting go
56. Right away, familiarly
57. Incident
58. Recess
60. Snack
61. Musical show
62. British general Thomas (1721-87)
63. Stated
64. More cunning
65. Greedy one

DOWN

1. One full of venom
2. Ran
3. Deceiver
4. One famous for his *Trees*
5. Excuse
6. Jules Verne hero
7. Musical instrument
8. __ Brothers
9. Purchaser's delight
10. Declare
11. Writer O'Flaherty
12. Benevolent and Protective Order
14. Come before
21. Elaborate solo
25. Pompous fool
26. *M*A*S*H* role
27. __ Gay; WWII plane
28. Cone droppers
29. Dunkirk dads
30. Word of disgust
31. In one's birthday suit
32. Biblical pronoun
33. More sensible
35. Gives one's okay
38. Contemptuous ones
39. Coming up
41. Suffix for claim or exult
42. French territories
44. Lent a hand
45. Usher
47. Trial locale
48. Little flaps
49. Land mass
50. Connected notes
52. 1st name for a daredevil
53. Mr. Strauss
54. One who built with gopherwood
55. __ dancer
59. Beer container

PUZZLE 27

ACROSS

1. Minor feud
5. Wolves
10. Sound of shock
14. Heidi's home
15. Sharp
16. Hipbones
17. Finn
18. Subject of the middle pages
20. Scottish weather condition
21. Newscaster Lindstrom and namesakes
22. Four Holy Roman Emperors
23. Actress born in Rome
25. Cockney dwelling
26. Friend
28. King Carl XVI Gustaf's subjects
31. Remove the lid
32. Greeting for Dolly
34. Bigwig, for short
36. Pallid
37. Vending machine purchases
38. Glass item
39. Gods: Lat.
40. Christmas decoration
41. Use an épée
42. Gorge
44. Londoner's sausage
45. Part of an addr.
46. Sea
47. State
50. Of a generation
51. Biologist's room
54. Bacteria killer
57. Head problem
58. Cards
59. Covering for 38 Across
60. 1975 Wimbledon champ
61. Fit together
62. Complaint to a proctologist
63. Dance movement

DOWN

1. Mineo and others
2. Make arrangements
3. Part of the United States
4. Recipe abbr.
5. Frillier
6. Indian, for one
7. Bakery purchases
8. Mel the Giant
9. Spot
10. Talented
11. "Thanks __ !"
12. Farm building
13. Tablets
19. Famous lover
21. __ school
24. All right
25. Hooters
26. Campus area
27. 1987 Indianapolis 500 champ
28. Murder
29. Matthew, Mark, Luke or John
30. Inasmuch as
32. Item for a golfer or a gopher
33. Section of a building
35. Gaze
37. Scoop holder
38. Famous 26 Across
40. Itchy problem
41. Do poorly
43. Disappear
44. Supports
46. Shower star
47. "Yes, __!"; polite response
48. Suffix for clear or sever
49. Residents: suff.
50. Common Latin abbr.
52. Longing
53. Impatient driver's sound
55. Uncanny sense
56. Fraternity letter
57. Spanish article

PUZZLE
28

ACROSS

1. Piece of clothing
6. Night sight
10. Calculating pros
14. Needing no encouragement
15. Sandwich
16. Rough, grating sound
17. Run and wed
18. Lunches
19. This: Sp.
20. Less familiar
22. Tantalizer
24. Discontinue
25. Crazy
26. __ oil
29. Do a grammatical exercise
30. Booth's victim
31. Adamant refusal
33. Commerce
37. Make sense of the written word
39. Peso spender
41. Strike
42. Fudd or Gantry
44. Nicknames for grandmas
46. __ You Lonesome Tonight?
47. VIP
49. Woman's clothing size
51. Makes
54. Editor's notation
55. Skate blade
56. Rhythmic flows
60. Footless creature
61. Manhandle
63. Big name in the Big Apple
64. Soccer great
65. 4840 square yards
66. Instruct
67. Scorch
68. Suffix for dry or shy
69. Exchanges for cash

DOWN

1. Notices
2. Lame
3. Mr. Stravinsky
4. Meal
5. Capital city
6. Unthinking followers
7. Sign of joy or sorrow
8. First host of House Party
9. List
10. Folders
11. Old hat
12. Garden bloom
13. Brief flash of light
21. Punctures
23. Once, once
25. Nobleman
26. __ for; tend
27. Guy with a mean brother
28. Word whose homonym has no a
29. Word with code or colony
32. Planet
34. __ Mountains; Kirghiz range
35. Game piece
36. Fencer's prop
38. Insistent one
40. Violated
43. By __ ; from memory
45. Picks
48. Language
50. Teacher's status
51. Vegas activity
52. Foreign money
53. __ Gay; WWII plane
54. Valleys
56. Unpedigreed pups
57. Ember
58. Lime on the rise
59. Kids for Charles & Di
62. Professional

1	2	3	4	5		6	7	8	9		10	11	12	13
14						15					16			
17						18					19			
20					21					22	23			
			24					25						
26	27	28					29							
30				31		32				33		34	35	36
37			38		39				40		41			
42				43		44				45		46		
			47		48				49		50			
51	52	53					54							
55						56					57	58	59
60					61	62				63				
64					65					66				
67					68					69				

ACROSS

1. Units of land
6. Bridge
10. Madrileño's home
14. Crinkled cloth
15. Record
16. Unwanted part
17. Gin's accompaniment
18. River flowing
    through Poland
19. Cappuccino containers
20. Is very hot
22. Apparition
24. Barnyard sound
25. Masculine names
26. Dances
29. Theater part
30. __ king
31. Temperature taker
33. Eliminate a boo-boo
37. Reside
39. Devour completely
41. Smelting refuse
42. For __ ; permanently
44. Wreck completely
46. __ pedestal;
    lovingly honored
47. Patient
49. In a chair
51. Raised one's voice
54. Catchall abbr.
55. Greeted
56. Process of trans-
    planting tissue
60. Unemployed
61. Toothed wheel
63. Burr
64. Sporting event
65. As a consequence
66. Sound of exertion
67. Georgia & others,
    formerly: abbr.
68. Raise
69. 1st name in cosmetics

DOWN

1. *As You Like It* divisions
2. Noisy flier
3. Monsieur Descartes
4. Closing section of a book
5. Part
6. Baby carrier?
7. Foxes' feet
8. Mock
9. Parts of teeth
10. Bunches
11. Home above
12. Hacienda herr
13. Leagues: abbr.
21. Follow
23. Man, for one
25. Deputy: abbr.
26. Jabber
27. Caught in __ ; found
    to be dishonest
28. Parishioners' section
29. Late actress Mary
32. Assigned a value to
34. "Thanks __ !"
35. Rational
36. Mild oath
38. Shoulder decorations
40. Noodles
43. Place
45. Foliage
48. Accountant's item
50. Sacred tables
51. Masonry wedges
52. Lower region
53. Football player
54. Miscalculation
56. Carried away: slang
57. In __ ; bored by routine
58. Away
59. Being: Sp.
62. Poet's word

1	2	3	4	5		6	7	8	9		10	11	12	13
14						15					16			
17						18					19			
20					21				22	23				
			24					25						
26	27	28					29							
30				31		32				33		34	35	36
37			38		39				40		41			
42				43		44				45		46		
			47		48				49		50			
51	52	53						54						
55						56					57	58	59
60					61	62				63			
64					65					66			
67					68					69			

ACROSS

1. Copy
4. Feminine title
9. Reach across
13. School subj.
15. Hard stone
16. Blanch
17. On the subject of
18. Forbidden acts
19. Uproar
20. Morse's brainchild
22. Roman date
23. __ bargain
24. Funny guy
26. Vocation
29. Novel supporters
34. Frighten
35. Loud noise
36. Island
37. Cleans linoleum
38. Beverage container
39. Crystallized mineral
40. Fraternity letter
41. Intimidate
42. Coupon user
43. Disappointed
45. Suns and Spurs: slang
46. Official, familiarly
47. Word with 1st-degree,
    2nd-degree or 3rd-degree
48. Bob
51. Fish homes
56. Land across the sea
57. Crown __ Vodka
58. Sweet treat
60. Poor area
61. Down provider
62. Permanent mark
63. Role for Dan Blocker
64. Boxes
65. Catch sight of

DOWN

1. Burgundy buddy
2. Breathe heavily
3. To be: Fr.
4. Part of a Nativity scene
5. Athenian assembly
   place
6. Mr. Andrews
7. Perched upon
8. Woven material
9. Carbonated drink
10. Rubber stamp for an
    accounting department
11. Skin lotion ingredient
12. Basketball team
14. Assistants
21. Type of school: abbr.
25. WWII Gen.
26. David and others
27. Hi in HI
28. Fast
29. Tasteless
30. Potter's kiln
31. Unsophisticated
32. Chopper
33. Deneb and Vega
35. Eye shade
38. Hooplas
39. Guns
41. Grade
42. Mother Teresa's garb
44. Imaginings
45. Doctors, hopefully
47. Lower
48. Meat concoction
49. Skagerrak seaport
50. One of 12 Popes
52. Witty remark
53. Meat inspection agcy.
54. Big __ ; french fries'
    accompaniments
55. Punish
59. Essay

1	2	3			4	5	6	7	8		9	10	11	12
13			14		15						16			
17					18						19			
	20			21							22			
			23						24	25				
26	27	28					29	30				31	32	33
34						35						36		
37					38						39			
40				41						42				
43			44						45					
			46					47						
48	49	50			51	52	53					54	55	
56					57						58			59
60					61						62			
63					64							65		

ACROSS

1. Feminine address
6. Fancy
10. "Howdy, __ !"; cowboy's greeting
14. San Antonio site
15. Make sharp
16. Take __ from; follow the suggestion of
17. Common high school subject, once
18. Doesn't exist
19. Use a towel
20. Do business
22. Like a good steak
24. State
25. Vision improvers
26. Pursuer
29. Like a smart aleck
30. Busy center
31. Scoundrel
33. Floor-length garments
37. Drinks
39. Entitled
41. Opposite of ruddy
42. __ Noster; The Lord's Prayer
44. Belief
46. Born
47. Duck
49. Business deal
51. Held in the arms
54. Ham's dad
55. Lots
56. Drill users
60. Discourteous
61. Ms. Adams
63. Stream
64. Summers abroad
65. Regretted
66. Money: slang
67. Maroon and scarlet
68. Turner and namesakes
69. Organic compound

DOWN

1. Beer ingredient
2. Having wings
3. Facts and figures
4. Nearly perfect mark
5. Loch Ness resident
6. What one
7. Multitude
8. Hotel
9. Quality of character
10. Store that thrives during a recession
11. Bitter substances
12. 100 paisas
13. Forest animals
21. Moses' brother
23. Sunrise location
25. Inexperienced
26. Fellow
27. Luau entertainment
28. Assist in wrongdoing
29. Angry person
32. Like a secured apartment complex
34. Band of delinquents
35. Nautical term
36. Prophet
38. Like some grapes
40. Evil spirit
43. Vex
45. British tradition
48. Treeless region
50. Horned mammals, for short
51. Kitchen utensil
52. Path
53. Put in
54. Must have
56. Expired
57. Opening
58. Prefix for prompter or scope
59. Heavenly object
62. Proper

PUZZLE
32

ACROSS

1. Large container
4. Wooden piece
8. Newscaster Sawyer
13. Capital city
14. Possess
15. Stranger
16. D __ David
17. Religious response
18. Openings
19. __ man
22. Author of
    The Purloined Letter
23. Fool
24. 10/31 option
26. Run the engine
29. Celtic soothsayers
32. Agreements
36. Singer
38. Plant part
39. Fictional captain
40. Official headdress
41. Handle: Lat.
42. __ Anderson
43. Heathen deity
44. Personal quality
45. Wraps
47. Pin-like?
49. Fudd or Gantry
51. Feline
56. School subject
58. Ladies in matching formals
61. Social division
63. Word with swipe or walk
64. Strike
65. Fall bloom
66. Like 2 or 10
67. Parts of icebergs
68. Home and second
69. Declaim violently
70. Nourish oneself

DOWN

1. Call on
2. __ acid
3. Gliding dance
4. Was generous
5. Young animal
6. State
7. Article of faith
8. Be unsteady
9. Words of commitment
10. Joyous family events
11. Cruel emperor
12. Gaelic
13. Can't keep up
20. Sponsorship
21. Zeal
25. Emanations
27. __ to rest; buried
28. Singer/pianist John
30. Measured amount
31. Now!
32. Friends
33. "...There'll be __ time
    in the old town..."
34. Paddlers
35. Short-term investment,
    familiarly
37. Prefix for vision
    or marketing
40. Stingy person
44. Tiny particle
46. Smoldering remains
48. Gone
50. Part of a staircase
52. Tend a roasting turkey
53. Eyelashes
54. Modify
55. Recipe abbrs.
56. Crusty formation
57. Toledo home
59. Aria performer
60. Ideal place
62. Ball support

PUZZLE 33

ACROSS
1. Prestigious award
6. Complaint to a plumber
10. Particle
14. Roger or Garry
15. Jot
16. Funeral conflagration
17. Awakener
18. Wheelless vehicle
19. Algerian seaport
20. Dependence
22. Transferred title to
    a third owner
24. Competes
25. Decides
26. Primps
29. __ metabolism
30. Name with Diamond
31. Unchanging
33. Most insignificant
37. In the center of
39. Stringed instrument
41. Pronounce indistinctly
42. Long
44. Distributes
46. Hombre's gold
47. Adjutants
49. Gave an exam
51. Entwined
54. Granary
55. Wrinkle remover
56. Hamilton and Burr
60. Urgent
61. Slumbering
63. Remove
64. Helper: abbr.
65. City in Kansas
66. Draw a new diagram
67. Unwanted portion
68. Form of *lie*
69. Fortunetellers

DOWN
1. Poet Khayyam
2. Shoe part
3. Fuel
4. Come
5. Lasts
6. Records
7. Part
8. Resident: suff.
9. San Diego __
10. Last Supper attendees
11. Alpine region
12. Papal scarf
13. Repairs
21. Egg holders
23. Common Latin abbr.
25. 1978 Nobel Peace
    Prize co-winner
26. *Hamlet* or *Macbeth*
27. Frost
28. Literary pseudonym
29. Nips
32. __ at; shot towards
34. Much
35. Positive response
36. Trampled
38. Police strategies
40. Make another knot
43. Source of water
    for 54 Down
45. Peter
48. Go off the track
50. Evening get-together
51. __ wave
52. Ascend
53. Like Odin and Thor
54. African nation
56. Salami supplier
57. Identical
58. Peter I or Ivan V
59. Months: abbr.
62. Accessory for the neck

1	2	3	4	5		6	7	8	9		10	11	12	13
14						15					16			
17						18					19			
20					21				22	23				
			24					25						
26	27	28					29							
30				31		32				33		34	35	36
37			38		39				40		41			
42				43		44				45		46		
			47		48				49		50			
51	52	53						54						
55						56						57	58	59
60					61	62					63			
64					65						66			
67					68						69			

ACROSS

1. Completely involved
5. Cut
9. Channing
14. General Bradley
15. Was carried along
16. Single
17. Soggy ground
18. "__ calling!"
19. Prominent
20. Continued effort
23. Bakery purchase
24. Be dishonest
25. Mary Todd's man
28. Gossip
32. Enjoy one's RV
34. Do a grammar exerc se
35. Talk wildly
37. Business transactic ۱
38. Horrors!
39. Ship
40. Commedia dell' __
41. Misplace
42. Trees
43. Church sections
44. Piece of playground
     equipment
46. Beginner
48. Units of measure: abbr.
49. Vowel follower
51. Arthur
52. Causing to be remembered
58. Asian nation
61. Residents: suff.
62. Inkling
63. Due
64. Canadian native
65. Hodgepodge
66. On edge
67. Transmit
68. Actress Carter

DOWN

1. Frolic
2. Pierre's girlfriend
3. Young salmon
4. Sins
5. Wants badly
6. Wander
7. Smell
8. Punitive
9. Dreaded disease
10. African lily
11. Nonsense
12. Numeral
13. Conducted
21. Emerald Isle
22. Saltpeter
25. Opposed
26. Word with egg or drum
27. Those French ladies
28. Like a saint
     in a painting
29. Eliminates errors
30. Musical number
31. Pulls hard
33. Movie based
     on a book
34. Neurological disorder
36. Sleeveless garment
39. Closer to the ground
43. Word with rug or code
45. Get even for
47. Handled badly
50. Stories
52. Items of cookware
53. Common French verb
54. Ending for six or seven
55. Unoccupied
56. Diamond
57. Liverpool slammer
58. Tiny amount
59. Wonder
60. Fastener

PUZZLE 35

ACROSS

1. Infant's ailment
6. French priest
10. Member of a Hindu sect
14. Amphitheater
15. Wild animal
16. Egyptian queen
17. Littlest
18. Emanation
19. Part of President Arthur's name
20. "Sunny and warm" or "Cloudy and cool"
22. Comfort
24. Not well-done
25. In the pink
26. Fight
29. Name for a tío
30. Ring great
31. One with Hansen's disease
33. Harpoon
37. Exigency
39. Lured
41. Fill
42. Curves
44. Less loony
46. Black or Red
47. *Silent Night*
49. Bug
51. Harms
54. Saga
55. Remains
56. Curtain rod concealers
60. By __ ; from memory
61. Cards
63. Holy scroll
64. U-__
65. 1 of 7 capital sins
66. Jagged
67. Editor's note
68. Ending for Nan or Ann
69. Used a sharp tool

DOWN

1. Young animal
2. Cookie
3. Play king
4. Put in
5. Derisive shout
6. Humiliate
7. Struggle
8. Keep out
9. Obliterated
10. Items on a seafood platter
11. __ ease; uncomfortable
12. Stacy
13. Toast topper
21. Spinning
23. Items used in pairs
25. Long-legged bird
26. Cause of distress
27. Potent potables
28. Neckwear
29. Part of a bicycle
32. Foreign currency
34. Direction
35. Fits to __
36. Stern
38. In a state of moral decline
40. Asian nation
43. Cook's herb
45. Connects
48. Realtor's transaction
50. Feminine title
51. Throwing game
52. Nearly
53. British bishop's item
54. Sample
56. Chest covering
57. Boast
58. Relaxation
59. Got rid of
62. Use a knife

1	2	3	4	5		6	7	8	9		10	11	12	13
14						15					16			
17						18					19			
20					21					22	23			
			24					25						
26	27	28					29							
30				31		32				33		34	35	36
37			38		39				40		41			
42				43		44				45		46		
			47		48				49		50			
51	52	53						54						
55							56					57	58	59
60					61	62				63				
64					65					66				
67					68					69				

ACROSS
1. Spoil
4. Washington runner
8. Walks back & forth
13. 100 centesimos
14. Shortly
15. Narrow passage
16. Years in Spain
17. Decorative nailhead
18. Barking animals
19. Contest entrants
22. Modern jet: abbr.
23. Item in a pencil box
24. Film holders
26. Baked loaves
29. Worshiped
32. Dry and crumbly
36. Swing around
38. Pinkish red
39. River in Italy
40. Candies
41. __ bene
42. Inlets
43. "Thanks __!"
44. Provide with a
    new crew
45. Vocation
47. Design again
49. Part of a pie
51. California Marine base
56. Suffix for fool or self
58. Head rooter
61. Sound of a horse's tail
63. To a __ ; exactly
64. Partial amount
65. Modern medical tool
66. Cake ingredient
67. Public transport
68. __ nous; confidentially
69. In a different way
70. Intuition

DOWN
1. Youth
2. Essence
3. Grates
4. Baker's product
5. Certain lobbyist
6. Form of arthritis
7. Witch's home
8. Went by
9. Stein contents
10. Teacher's milieu
11. Slimy swimmers
12. Method: abbr.
13. Frilly edging
20. Uncanny
21. Raises
25. Pa Cartwright
27. Bad
28. Sombrero wearer
30. This: Sp.
31. College official
32. __ Antony
33. Assam silkworm
34. One opposed to
    all government
35. Aesop's hare
37. Diminutive ending
40. Wetland
44. Dramatic character
46. Card game
48. Eliminate
50. Taunt
52. One of the senses
53. Fragrances
54. Draw out a new route
55. __ , Utah
56. Isolated land
57. Word with song or dive
59. Catchall abbr.
60. Meth. and Episc.
62. Indian weight

PUZZLE
37

ACROSS

1. Get up
6. Carpet layer's computation
10. Periods
14. Thick soup
15. Look like
16. Name for a Spanish girl
17. Go in
18. Total destruction
20. Start of a U. S. state capital
21. Jungle beasts
23. Lauder
24. Short life stories
25. Word on a banana
27. Do a shoemaker's job
30. Skimpy garment
31. Holder of groceries
34. Bismarck, for one
35. Beverage
36. Feminine one: Sp.
37. Cafe employees
41. Excellent test mark
42. Ram
43. Jim Nabors' role
44. Uncanny sense
45. Strip
46. Raised platforms
48. Hodgepodge
49. Encyclopedia
50. Blue
53. Leafy vegetable
54. Expert
57. Discharges
60. Of a branch
   of the service
62. __ , Alaska
63. Run
64. Thirst quencher
65. Digits
66. Ending for cigar or novel
67. Factions

DOWN

1. Hurried
2. Melody
3. Crafts
4. Born
5. Throw off the track
6. Residue
7. Cars of yesterday
8. Moray
9. Latin learner's verb
10. Wipe away
11. Sound defeat
12. South African fox
13. Satisfy
19. __ disease;
   intestinal problem
22. One who wrote *The Raven*
24. Coarse person
25. Chops well
26. __ about;
   approximately
27. TV's *The Trials of
   __ O'Neill*
28. Group characteristics
29. Condescend
30. Example
31. Warnings for boatmen
32. Leg part
33. Ozone and oxygen
35. Sobs
38. Candles
39. Silver and uranium
40. Role for Ron Howard
46. Monetary unit: abbr.
47. Fixes
48. Sea divider
49. Flavor
50. Copper
51. Melville novel
52. Fruit
53. Shoelace problem
54. Zealous
55. Candy shape
56. Club
58. Ending for favor or graph
59. Scrap
61. Jackie's second

PUZZLE 38

1	2	3	4	5		6	7	8	9		10	11	12	13
14						15					16			
17						18				19				
20				21	22					23				
			24					25	26					
27	28	29					30					31	32	33
34						35						36		
37				38	39						40			
41				42							43			
44				45					46	47				
			48					49						
50	51	52					53					54	55	56
57					58	59					60	61		
62					63						64			
65					66						67			

ACROSS

1. Patient's need, for short
4. Entree choice
7. Hinter
11. Solos
13. Oman's location
15. Mayberry resident
16. Doing as well as one can with
19. Starter
20. Jumbo
21. Word with drum or mark
23. Tres divided by tres
24. Baby's favorite seat
27. Wicked one
30. Con artist's plot
34. Romeo
36. Half of a funny duo of past decades
38. Genetic carrier
39. Alpine crest
40. Mich.'s neighbor
41. Traveling salesman
43. Deface
44. Split grammatically
46. Ponders
47. Picnic spoilers
49. Looks intently
51. McKinley & Whitney: abbr.
52. H, in Greece
54. Pres. Hafez al-Assad's nation: abbr.
56. In ___ ; not present
61. Literary device
66. Outwits
68. ___ Fitzgerald
69. River in Belgium
70. Pub order
71. Pack away
72. Poet's monogram
73. Suffix for differ or exist

DOWN

1. Catch
2. Be attracted to
3. First son
4. Accessory
5. Tennis pro
6. Manner
7. Universe
8. Dependent upon
9. 4 that sometimes follow A
10. Penalty assigners, for short
11. I love: Lat.
12. Dagger
14. Be plentiful
17. Former student, for short
18. Type of eagle
22. Take back as an employee
24. Long Range Navigation, familiarly
25. Turn away
26. Favorite
28. Parsonage
29. Dictates
31. Toothpaste
32. Boleyn and Bancroft
33. Front porch items
34. Dalai ___
35. Joseph P. Kennedy II, for one: abbr.
37. Edible tuber
42. Part of the mouth
45. Opposite of concern
48. Vacillate
50. Method: abbr.
53. Blaster's substance
55. Word of disgust
56. 4, 5, and 6, for kindergartners
57. Waist item
58. French commune
59. Suffix for sand or wind
60. Fortas and Vigoda
62. Head of France
63. Numbered club
64. Put to flight
65. Salamander
67. Prior to

PUZZLE 39

ACROSS
1. Cargo
5. French cleric
9. O. Henry, to Porter
14. Name for 2 of
    Henry VIII's wives
15. Explosion
16. Shape metal
17. Sweet treat
18. Part
19. Atlanta, in the
    1991 World Series
20. Costumed child's words
23. Aunt Juanita or Aunt Lupe
24. Orange-colored edible
25. Downed
28. Molar tooth
32. College class
34. One lacking freedom
35. Low
37. Dryer
38. Type size
39. Chest material
40. Bet
41. Underground passage
42. Mars' counterpart
43. Viper
44. Feel bitter about
46. Ballroom dances: var.
48. Suffix for cold or calm
49. Poetic contraction
51. Nothing
52. Was an indicator of
58. Performed
61. Piece of bacon
    or concrete
62. Concern
63. Edible mushroom
64. Cash register drawer
65. Oven
66. Slyly derisive
67. Pintail duck
68. Editor's notation

DOWN
1. Survive
2. __ about; approximately
3. *The King* __
4. Make inoperable
5. Overseas
6. Inconsiderate one
7. Leave quickly
8. __ board
9. On fire
10. Pillage
11. Not-too-popular U. S. agcy.
12. Generation
13. To be: Sp.
21. Cows
22. Avid
25. Blake of *Gunsmoke*
26. Uses one of
    the senses
27. Penetrate
28. Moves smoothly
29. Bigot
30. Word with who or when
31. Horseman
33. Motorists' obstructions
34. Extra
36. Whip
39. __ to; serve
43. Hemmed in by
45. Head: colloq.
47. Incompetent
50. Catches some Zs
52. Nourish
53. Svelte
54. Vigorous
55. Cool one's heels
56. Perry Mason's creator
57. Car blemish
58. Mornings, for short
59. Felon
60. Numerical prefix

ACROSS

1. College major
4. Without ___ ;
   happy-go-lucky
9. Have the leading role
13. Refreshing spot
15. Meat
16. Take on
17. Edible tuber
18. Give a formal address
19. Sign
20. Australia
22. Interpret
23. Isolated
24. Gained
26. Insist
29. Unmarried one
34. Castle
35. Burn rapidly
36. Samuel's mentor
37. Liz's third
38. Chatter
39. Times
40. Union's foe in the
    Civil War: abbr.
41. Hot under the collar
42. Sticky stuff
43. Unable to care for oneself
45. Teaching or engineering
46. Luth. or Meth.
47. Primary
48. Wander
51. Characters on *L. A. Law*
56. 11 and 12, for preteens
57. Scottish clan chief
58. Official imprint
60. Distribute
61. Gourmand
62. Fable
63. Bothersome person
64. Hangs around
65. Skelton

DOWN

1. Pertinent
2. Word with block or side
3. Valencia victim
4. Be plentiful
5. Chili con ___
6. School: abbr.
7. By ___ ; from memory
8. Give strength to
9. Word with Bermuda
   or boxer
10. 1:10 or 2:20
11. Region
12. Split
14. Valley
21. 25 Down minus
    25 Down
25. Numeral
26. Moat
27. Uneven
28. Religious article
29. Wooden pieces
30. Spread
31. Brief
32. Thrill
33. Part of a staircase
35. Lingerie shop
    purchases
38. Bishops
39. Sincere
41. Tahiti, for one
42. Sign of bursitis
44. Determined
    beforehand
45. Concerned people
47. Dough
48. Inclined surface
49. Arch style
50. November honorees
52. Pronoun
53. See ya!
54. Item on an
    almanac cover
55. Shopper's delight
59. Pioneered

ACROSS

1. Courtroom mallet
6. Dramatic opener
10. __ away; store
14. Still with us
15. No longer with us
16. Center
17. Lawgiver
18. Faithful
20. Vast expanse
21. Eyes
23. Muffin toppers
24. Beverage
25. Pond scum
27. Calling
30. Leo
31. Make a lap
34. Devastate
35. Pacific island group
36. Self-esteem
37. 119 days before Halloween
41. Tours tourist time
42. Covered with a climbing plant
43. Parishioners' area
44. Div. of a former nation
45. Tears
46. Gave one's views
48. Anemic
49. Glider
50. Proofreader's mark
53. __ down; resign
54. Tournament for Nicklaus: abbr.
57. Impasse
60. Kilt pattern
62. Up and __ ; stirring
63. Smell
64. Punishment given in *The Man Without a Country*
65. Skedaddles
66. Karol Wojtyla, today
67. Brooks

DOWN

1. Shapely legs
2. __ vera
3. Traveler's item
4. Genesis figure
5. Tenant
6. Reptile
7. Open circles
8. Small amount
9. Amin
10. La __ ; opera house
11. Bear
12. Cookie jar item
13. Gets hitched
19. Liqueur
22. Suffix for mountain or ballad
24. Nota __
25. __ toward; shot at
26. Diving bird
27. Wails
28. Relations
29. Equestrian
30. Serves bouillabaisse
31. Automobile
32. "__ at the office."
33. Trifled
35. Attack from hiding
38. Hook, for one
39. Malicious
40. __ , Oklahoma
46. Spanish shout
47. Seasoning
48. Skins
49. Cubic meter
50. Former rulers' title
51. Aleutian island
52. Picnic spoiler
53. Octagon word
54. Milker's need
55. Bass' organ
56. Fruity concoctions
58. Floor cleaner
59. Bustle
61. This clue

1	2	3	4	5		6	7	8	9		10	11	12	13
14						15					16			
17						18			19					
20				21	22					23				
			24					25	26					
27	28	29					30					31	32	33
34						35						36		
37				38	39					40				
41				42							43			
44				45					46	47				
			48					49						
50	51	52					53					54	55	56
57					58	59				60	61			
62					63					64				
65					66					67				

ACROSS
1. Shiny on top
5. Forward sections
10. Engrossed
14. African lily
15. Permitted
16. Lake tribe
17. Roarer
18. Texas athlete
19. Entry
20. Salad ingredient
22. Antelopes
24. Suffix for expert or treat
25. Crawler
26. Use the other end of the pencil
29. Equip
30. See 15 Across
34. Earth
35. Isolated piece of land
36. Redistribute cards
37. __ Maria
38. Kidnaps
40. Gun owners' org.
41. Threaten
43. Common verb
44. Tragic destiny
45. Move suddenly
46. Porker's home
47. British princess
48. __ pie
50. Reptile
51. Get well
54. __ of; throw out
58. Nostrils' detection
59. Cut off
61. Always
62. Dinner accompaniment
63. Spoil
64. Los Angeles __
65. Beginning
66. Word with black or lock
67. Thin opening

DOWN
1. Dance
2. Tell __ ; be dishonest
3. Money: slang
4. One who says "Open wide"
5. Locale
6. Heed one's alarm
7. Time to plan a masquerade party: abbr.
8. Electrician's task
9. Opening, in plants
10. Feasted
11. Russian sea
12. __ bread
13. Pegs
21. Take advantage of
23. Stacks
25. Place
26. Cheeses
27. Fix firmly
28. Public building
29. Free
31. Columbus' home
32. Exodus figure
33. Pack animal
35. Presidential nickname
36. Address abbr.
38. Part where Juliet makes plans to elope with Romeo
39. Boo-hoo
42. Like a Brinks truck
44. Pampers
46. Shriek
47. Colombian couple
49. Fits snugly
50. Joyous event
51. Squabbles
52. Ms. Adams
53. Rocky road holder
54. Fender-bender memento
55. Shape
56. Prefix for circle or private
57. Formerly
60. Square root of XLIX

PUZZLE
43

ACROSS

1. Space
4. Unruly tot
7. Forbidden: var.
11. Went public with
13. Hombre's parlor
15. Blind as __
16. Alaska's neighbor
19. Grandparents
20. Bicuspids' neighbors
21. Aristotle's H
23. Home: abbr.
24. Hunter
27. Lean
30. Run
34. Cause one to say
    "Deja vu"
36. Russian city on
    the Bug River
38. Address abbr.
39. Overact
40. Rink surface
41. Stranger
43. Calendar page: abbr.
44. Punished
46. Be filled with desire
47. Like the Nile
49. __ well; is a good omen
51. Scrap
52. Generation
54. Like, hippie-style
56. Laxative ingredient
61. Skim
66. Pompidou's predecessor
68. 13th word of
    The Lord's Prayer
69. Prague resident
70. Feudal lord
71. Caustic substances
72. Scottish uncle
73. Social event

DOWN

1. "It's a __ !"
2. Withered
3. Rose
4. Suffix for child or boor
5. Spice
6. Stratagem
7. Easiest to handle
8. Parisian priest
9. Fisherman's need
10. State
11. Buchanan's successor,
    to friends
12. Distressful
14. Cautions
17. Jets, familiarly
18. Western Indian
22. Pale one
24. Allegro or andante
25. Oak dropping
26. Still
28. Curved
29. Was dependent upon
31. Speeder's nemesis
32. Obvious
33. Shorebird
34. True
35. __ room
37. Gift for a child
42. "Gloria in excelsis __ !"
45. Puts down
48. Classes
50. Make music without
    an instrument
53. Episc. or Cath.
55. Score for Orr
56. V x V x V x V x II
57. Nautical greeting
58. Checkers
59. Small land mass
60. With 67 Down,
    famous couple
62. Night: Fr.
63. Get away
64. Marsh growth
65. Letter
67. See 60 Down

ACROSS

1. Show approval
5. Robert or Jack
10. Pet shop purchases
14. Capital city
15. Roper's event
16. Substitute product
17. Land of bliss
18. Perfect
19. Tumble
20. WWII era
22. Smacked
24. French pronoun
25. Puts on the bulletin board
26. Beast of burden
29. Shallow container
30. Slightest
34. Sashes
35. Establish
36. Annual celebration
37. Sailor's milieu
38. Accusations
40. Onassis
41. Native Mexican food
43. Word with motor
    or vegetable
44. Fruit
45. __ acid
46. Lodge
47. __ to be; looks like
48. Hot spots
50. Monkey
51. Praise
54. Item on a seafood platter
58. Musical number
59. Ending for be or under
61. Let up
62. One who played
    Ethel Mertz's neighbor
63. Loose
64. Leave the ground
65. Weaver's reed
66. Brain passages
67. Word with shot or dragon

DOWN

1. 𝄞
2. Resort island
3. Mexican's neighbor: abbr.
4. Undergarments
5. Burger accompaniments
6. Linear measures
7. Lyrical work
8. Fall
9. Motorists' charges
10. Lifeless ones
11. Leaning
12. Prefix for type or cast
13. Convinced
21. Not well
23. Traveler's aid
25. Patrick and Bridget,
    for Ireland
26. Start of a Central
    American nation
27. Perpendicular to a
    ship's keel
28. Dolphins' home
29. Veggie
31. __ of Two Cities
32. Antitoxin
33. Edges
35. Pronoun
36. Sea creature
38. Pungent spice
39. Triumphant card player's cry
42. Peculiarity
44. Kitchen implements
46. Begin a paragraph
47. Baden-Baden, for one
49. Tedium
50. Is sore
51. Public vehicles
52. Said
53. Unit of distance
54. Recipe direction
55. Form of *lie*
56. Greek peak
57. Tiny sound
60. Broke bread

1	2	3	4		5	6	7	8	9		10	11	12	13
14					15						16			
17					18						19			
20				21				22		23				
			24				25							
26	27	28				29				30		31	32	33
34					35				36					
37				38				39				40		
41			42				43				44			
45					46					47				
			48		49				50					
51	52	53						54				55	56	57
58					59		60				61			
62					63						64			
65					66						67			

ACROSS

1. Reptile
4. Five diamonds
9. Covenant
13. Moved smoothly
15. Member of the royalty
16. Bylaw
17. Cabbage's cousin
18. Fragrance
19. Native American
20. Cone-shaped device
22. Foolish ones
23. Fully developed
24. Appropriate
26. Real estate transaction
29. Fried batter cakes
34. ☞ ☞ ☞
35. Fry
36. Give permission to
37. Arch style
38. Violet
39. Walking aid
40. Word before a
    maiden name
41. Pine Tree State
42. Mistake
43. In a straying manner
45. Part of some backyards
46. Poker term
47. Winter sight
48. Clasp
51. Newspaper feature
56. Bicycled
57. Rejuvenate
58. Dye ingredient
60. Intestinal parts
61. Audacity
62. Overdue
63. Cherished
64. Jet's advantage
65. Darn

DOWN

1. Inquire
2. Door's noise
3. Mound
4. Cool dessert
5. Shaper
6. Biblical preposition
7. Irishman's name
8. Important factor in
   longevity
9. Adjusted beforehand
10. Personal emanation

12. Pieces of wood that are
    pressed into the turf
14. Humiliate
21. Is not in the pink
25. Early Coloradan
26. River in France
27. Raring to go
28. Haughty expression
29. Seat
30. Trick
31. Oxlike antelope
32. Name for a femme
33. Strict
35. Oars' alternative
38. Beginning sewer's needs
39. Friendly
41. 6, on a telephone
42. 1934 heavyweight champ
44. Show up
45. Shone
47. McQueen
48. Word with lock or iron
49. Function
50. "What's the big __ ?"
52. Very low
53. Regarding
54. Woeful exclamation
55. Instrument of old
59. Request for a
    bowl of milk

1	2	3			4	5	6	7	8		9	10	11	12
13			14		15						16			
17					18						19			
	20			21						22				
		23					24	25					
26	27	28				29	30				31	32	33
34					35					36			
37				38					39			
40				41					42			
43			44					45				
		46				47					
48	49	50			51	52	53				54	55	
56				57					58			59
60				61					62			
63				64					65			

ACROSS

1. Make merry
6. Fat
10. Fairly good report card
14. Tie
15. Early Ron Howard role
16. Place
17. Robert and Elizabeth
18. Bullies
20. Suffix for computer
or Vietnam
21. Blessed femmes: abbr.
23. Analyze ore
24. Beverages
25. Spunky
27. Cause to remember
30. Like a bird
31. Suffix for elector
or compassion
34. Abbr. that occurs at
the end of a sentence
35. River in Europe
36. Maria Shriver's uncle
37. Showing indecision
41. Billfold item
42. Let up
43. In a different way
44. Nuns: abbr.
45. Australian birds
46. Virginia and others
48. Celtic language
49. Eye secretion
50. Peer
53. Minerals
54. Part of a wk.
57. Burrowing mammal
60. Animal with a snout
62. Untrue statements
63. Relish tray item
64. Get around
65. Sound
66. Gem
67. Stupid

DOWN

1. Inconsiderate
2. Son of Seth
3. Wicked
4. Une saison
5. Reduce
6. Ear parts
7. Spring parts: abbr.
8. Hombre's fishing spot
9. Condensation
10. Holy
11. Prejudice
12. Second letter
13. Working
19. Monkeys' container?
22. Mite
24. Work the soil
25. Beg
26. British countess' hubby
27. Relaxes
28. Anesthetic
29. Principal conduits
30. Residue
31. Like Pisa's tower
32. Present, for one
33. Works on the lawn
35. Take ___ ; disagree
38. Had a sly look
39. Ham's accompaniments
40. Period of time
46. Behold
47. Took a bite of
48. Get rid of
49. Folklore creature
50. 1st word in a U. S.
state capital
51. Bee Gees, for one
52. Word from the nave
53. Earthenware jar
54. Stretch across
55. Helps
56. Pine
58. Altar words
59. Facial feature
61. ___ *Maria*

PUZZLE
47

ACROSS

1. Con game
5. Handle: Lat.
9. Student's assignment
14. Lacking vividness
15. Ray
16. Knowledgeable
17. One who acts
    like another
18. Italian dough
19. Prices
20. Studying mainly one
    part of a subject
23. Smoothing tool
24. Pilot's direction: abbr.
25. ABC's competitor
28. Surface layers
32. Skillful
34. Useful rope
35. Town in Buckinghamshire
37. Exterior: pref.
38. Italian city
39. Saw
40. Carol
41. Singer/songwriter Billy
42. Black: Fr.
43. Worship
44. Stop
46. Tidies
48. Draft board: abbr.
49. One on Pedro's family tree
51. Show __
52. Skeptics
58. Island nation
61. 1st-century poet
62. Spreadable edible
63. Due
64. Grape holder
65. Branch of the service:
    abbr.
66. Eye color determinants
67. Club
68. Poison remedies

DOWN

1. Offerings of some
   apartment complexes
2. Li'l Abner's creator
3. Sailor's direction
4. Retail business
5. Burning
6. Diamond
7. Woman's garment
8. Astonish
9. Deserved
10. Decorative, hanging chain
11. Used a chair
12. Form of *be*
13. Okay
21. Scheme
22. Senseless
25. Insect stage
26. Mean dogs
27. Broke a commandment
28. Parts of some caps
29. Diners
30. Change the room scheme
31. Spot
33. Arranged meeting
34. Princes
36. Cinderella's stepmother
    or the Big Bad Wolf
39. Pros' opponents
43. In __ ; even
45. Burns
47. Stays
50. Over
52. Prime Minister Poul
    Schluter, for one
53. Corrupt
54. Connection
55. Otherwise
56. Word with end or admiral
57. Piece of furniture
58. Engage in an
    outdoor exercise
59. Mixture of fear
    and wonder
60. Sharp object

ACROSS

1. Persian Gulf War missile
5. Vice
10. Latvian capital
14. Score too few points
15. Come afterward
16. Actress Moran
17. Augury
18. Make reparation
19. King or queen
20. Clergymen
22. Goes to
24. Conjunctions
25. Was sore
26. Meager
29. Put forth effort
30. Peewee
34. Reduce
35. Lobbying group, for short
36. Ledger column
37. S. A. nation
38. Gruesome
40. Decompose
41. Of the nervous system
43. Female animal
44. Floor piece
45. Guide
46. Miss, coming out
47. Gladness
48. Mideast breads
50. Cochlea's location
51. Kangaroo, for one
54. Side by side
58. Ein und ein und ein
59. Bitter
61. In the matter of
62. Lab item
63. French pension
64. Neckwear
65. Lounging
66. Curved
67. Dummies

DOWN

1. Make a mess
2. Near-death condition
3. __ up; spends
4. Part of a tooth
5. Is apprehensive about
6. Insects
7. Org. founded in 1941
8. Craziness
9. Items cleaned, filled and pulled
10. Goes back
11. Oil exporter
12. Surround
13. "No ifs, __ or..."
21. Poet's contraction
23. Opposite of wordy
25. Video game lovers' paradises
26. Snaps up
27. Insertion mark
28. Dispute
29. Toe's predecessor, in game name
31. Outre
32. Wrap
33. Organic compound
35. Comrade
36. Common verb
38. Main character in *West Side Story*
39. Hope
42. Adder
44. Indications of imminent danger
46. Troupe member
47. Means of transportation
49. Regal item
50. Lessened
51. CCIII doubled
52. Parched
53. Loud ringing
54. *Laugh-In* regular
55. 11 Down's location
56. Word with children or mother
57. Pitch
60. Business letter abbr.

1	2	3	4		5	6	7	8	9		10	11	12	13
14					15						16			
17					18						19			
20				21				22		23				
			24				25							
26	27	28				29				30		31	32	33
34					35				36					
37				38				39				40		
41			42				43				44			
45						46				47				
			48		49				50					
51	52	53					54				55	56	57
58					59		60				61			
62					63						64			
65					66						67			

ACROSS

1. Juice flavor
6. Broad, thick piece
10. High school class
14. Star of TV's *Alice*
15. Nearly midnight
16. Word in Texas' nickname
17. Colder
18. Opinion
19. __ Major
20. Sleeping places
22. Maiden
24. Helpful hint
25. Opposite of replenish
26. Judicial pounders
29. Western event
30. Pres. Johnson's
    predecessor
31. Greek porticoes
33. Fem. titles
37. Lose one's footing
39. Pack rat
41. Valley
42. __ code
44. Car
46. Charge
47. "He is __ !";
    Easter phrase
49. Roof support
51. Facial features,
    for some
54. Vegas activity
55. Blake of *Gunsmoke*
56. Dawns
60. Only
61. Fly
63. Type of 49 Across
64. Role in *Frankenstein*
65. Award
66. Run to Gretna Green
67. Girls' nicknames
68. 15th-century
    ocean crosser
69. Intelligence

DOWN

1. Smooth-talking
2. Asian or Caucasian
3. Fervent
4. White House resident
   (1853-57)
5. __ in; joins
6. Slippery matter
7. Boys
8. Lunched
9. Like some evening bags
10. Unscrupulous
    rent collector
11. Mount
12. First stage
13. Noted clergyman
21. Removes forcibly
23. Mocks
25. Gave medicine to
26. Sound of astonishment
27. Qualified
28. Part of the circulatory
    system
29. Poe subject
32. Places of welcome relief
34. Heaviest of 41
35. Nautical term
36. Augur
38. Spouses
40. Less common
43. Fibbed
45. Pram pushers
48. Spring
50. Weakness
51. Oliver Twist, e.g.
52. Last
53. Home run champ
54. North __
56. Common street name
57. Bright light
58. Openings
59. Pintail duck
62. Broad sash

PUZZLE
50

ACROSS

1. Peaks: abbr.
4. Facial covering
8. Book parts
13. Terse
14. __ *Karenina*
15. Showed again
16. Solo
17. Mix
18. Got up
19. City near Pompeii
22. Notice
23. Jacket part
24. Youths
26. Blue-pencil
29. Fight sites
32. Accomplices: abbr.
36. Girls' nicknames
38. Article of clothing
39. Facts
40. Sky sight
41. ¿Cómo __ ?;
     How are you?
42. Is off
43. Antitoxins
44. Criminal activity
45. Snoozing period
47. Window part
49. Closes securely
51. *Like this type*
56. Existed
58. Ape
61. Pivotal
63. In __ ; mired by
     routine
64. Soothsayer's sign
65. Type
66. Ferris wheel
67. Move quickly
68. Trimmed
69. Sharp
70. Suffix for murder or poet

DOWN

1. Wall covering
2. Nonsense: slang
3. Old
4. Gathered together
5. Prefix for thesis or septic
6. Angry mood
7. 1/24, to a jeweler
8. Contemplative's specialty
9. Of flying: pref.
10. Lack of refinement
11. Alleviate
12. Pointed weapon
13. Fires: colloq.
20. Preceding periods
21. Let
25. __ mind!; Forget it!
27. Unemployed
28. __ into; attacks:
     colloq.
30. Concerning
31. Laurel
32. Beverages
33. Floor-length garment
34. Emphasizing
35. Café au lait container
37. __ B'rith; international
     Jewish organization
40. 8 Down, for King David
44. Chorale member
46. Followed
48. Use one of the senses
50. Vivacity
52. Charged electrode
53. Religious men
54. Brain channels
55. Coin
56. Salary
57. Chopped
59. U. S. body of water
60. Mannerless
62. Present verb

ACROSS

1. Monroe's successor
6. School event
10. Make a mess
14. Fabric with a wavy pattern
15. Dinner course
16. Feline
17. Accessory
18. One with a breathing disorder
20. 6 Across attendees: abbr.
21. Saga
23. Andean ridge
24. Pretense
25. Concocted
27. Lathe
30. Appear
31. Brazilian gentleman
34. Fictional estate
35. Earth: Lat.
36. __ pedestal; lovingly honored
37. Irritates
41. __ Z; full gamut
42. Bread spread
43. Oman's location
44. Word with cent or chance
45. God of love
46. Bar
48. Beverage container
49. Soothe
50. Theater part
53. Range
54. Sound of support
57. Loyal
60. Shun a big ceremony
62. Lame
63. Singer
64. Negative word
65. Magazine title
66. Inert gas
67. Levels

DOWN

1. Elec. units
2. Gloomy
3. Haughtiness
4. Fem. title
5. Be furious
6. 1 of 150
7. Kennedy
8. Not "safe"
9. Driver's speed: abbr.
10. Lean
11. Stringed instrument
12. Delete
13. Walk the floor
19. Lunatic
22. Swiss river
24. Springs
25. Start of a holiday greeting
26. Prefix for ballistics or dynamics
27. Belt
28. High: Fr.
29. Shady place
30. Clothes maker
31. Use a divining rod
32. Happy as a lark
33. Central American Indian language
35. Caruso or Pavarotti
38. Melted
39. __ plate
40. Was generous
46. Type of dance
47. Express acceptance
48. Opposite of depress
49. Mr. John
50. Arthur with a racket
51. Eur. language
52. Peddle
53. On the subject of
54. Wander
55. Copycat
56. Pronoun
58. Cooler
59. 46 Across order
61. Garland

1	2	3	4	5		6	7	8	9		10	11	12	13
14						15					16			
17						18				19				
20				21	22					23				
		24					25	26					
27	28	29					30					31	32	33
34					35						36			
37			38	39						40			
41			42						43				
44			45				46	47				
		48				49						
50	51	52				53					54	55	56
57				58	59				60	61			
62				63				64			
65				66				67			

ACROSS

1. Uncle __
4. Golfer's hazard
8. Thrill
13. Baby's word
14. Chaplin's wife
15. Star-crossed lover
16. Zest for life
17. Colors
18. Fluttering tree
19. Justices of the Peace
22. __ Missouri
23. Conceive
24. Highly skilled
26. Zeus and Hera's kid
29. Long-running
    Broadway play
32. County in Texas
36. Ending for check or room
38. Part of some
    feminine names
39. Language: abbr.
40. Ohio, for one
41. Entree choice
42. Poetess Teasdale
43. Object
44. Nickname for a president
45. Alleged
47. Ship's pole
49. Belief
51. Amiable
56. Cheerleader's shout
58. Capable of being
    sailed across
61. Soap source
63. Reduce
64. Agony
65. Better
66. Someone __ ;
    another person
67. Parts of 12 Down
68. SATs
69. __ straight;
    informs properly
70. Hissing sound

DOWN

1. Dieter's lunch
2. Saw
3. Rage
4. Appear unsteady
5. Hit the ceiling
6. __ and the King of Siam
7. Noodles
8. Rubber end
9. Spanish article
10. Cut off
11. Wooden pegs
12. Geological cycles
13. Ms. Moore
20. Symbol of Judaism
21. Lawn tool
25. Irk
27. Discharge
28. Puts away for later
30. South African town
31. Snakelike
32. Miss
33. Smell __ ;
    suspect trickery
34. Races
35. Ebb
37. Not perm.
40. Horseman
44. Uno y dos
46. Passes into
48. __ with; suits
50. Music lover's purchases
52. Collar areas
53. Steel beams
54. Otherwise known as
55. Eye part
56. Simplest of transports
57. Confidante
59. Glen
60. Once
62. __ alone; not to mention

PUZZLE 53

ACROSS
1. Water vapor
6. Round: abbr.
10. Fraud
14. Stadium
15. Skating rink
16. Related account
17. Stolen
18. Punctuation mark
20. 23rd letters, flipped
21. Phooey!
23. Ready for battle
24. Confused jumble
25. Beget
27. On the land
30. Play people
31. Auxiliary verb
34. Fish-eating mammal
35. Fine netting
36. Again, in music
37. Generosity
41. Omega
42. Iniquities
43. Nautical term
44. Susan of *L. A. Law*
45. Lean
46. Tends the lawn
48. Paving substances
49. Opposite of goofy
50. Saharan transport
53. Marriage symbol
54. Item for sitters only
57. Left high and dry
60. Unrestrained
62. Folksinger Seeger
63. Knotty swelling
64. Rub out
65. Bench piece
66. Parts of psyches
67. Less risky

DOWN
1. Quench
2. Parking lot-to-airport
   transportation
3. Noises heard when a
   wimp sees a mouse
4. One: Scot.
5. Way
6. Expenses
7. Burl
8. Crash into
9. One-quarter of DCIV
10. Shopper's destination
11. Weather prediction
12. African flower
13. On the __ ; healing
19. Transported
22. Exploit
24. Shape
25. Preservatives
26. Small land surrounded
    by the ocean
27. Questioned
28. English Channel feeder
29. Conveniently located
30. Like little
    Shirley Temple
31. White poplar
32. One who ascends
33. Alphabet characters
35. Opposite of heads
38. Announce the arrival of
39. Word with for or which
40. Man's nickname
46. Sickly looking
47. Formations that are
    sometimes acute
48. Religious principle
49. Take __ ; show partiality
50. Bonnets
51. Fourth person
52. __ Hari
53. Make over
54. Bakery purchase
55. South African fox
56. Word with pressure
    or group
58. .36524 + .63476
59. Holiday party offering
61. __ pro nobis; pray for us

PUZZLE
54

1	2	3	4	5		6	7	8	9		10	11	12	13
14						15					16			
17						18				19				
20					21	22					23			
			24						25	26				
27	28	29					30					31	32	33
34						35					36			
37				38	39					40				
41				42							43			
44				45					46	47				
			48					49						
50	51	52					53					54	55	56
57				58	59				60	61				
62					63					64				
65					66					67				

ACROSS

1. Small weight
5. Actor's place
10. Tempted one
14. Character
15. Lower region
16. Letter closing
17. Make __ ; gamble
18. Sailor's direction
19. Currier's partner
20. Protects
22. Events on a paper's business page
24. Source of caviar
25. Nobleman
26. Trainee
29. Enjoyment
30. Meaning
34. Felt terrible about
35. Container
36. Tranquilize
37. Live
38. Notices
40. Sun deity
41. Attic
43. Promotional write-ups
44. Word with tall or fairy
45. Weather condition
46. Appropriate
47. Runner
48. Crosses out
50. Beverage
51. Long-running Broadway play
54. Periods of time
58. Monthly payment: abbr.
59. Facilitates
61. Donahue
62. Missing
63. In stitches
64. Suffixes for velvet and eight
65. Common contraction
66. One-armed bandits
67. Plant part

DOWN

1. Homecoming attendee
2. Garment
3. Hebrew letter
4. Like short-term parking
5. Color
6. Sole attachments
7. Foofaraw
8. Like Beethoven
9. Organic compound
10. Straightened
11. Type of bird
12. State
13. Disarray
21. Negative word
23. American Beauties
25. Pieces of furniture
26. Mountaineer's hazards
27. Of one of the senses
28. Name in farm equipment
29. Like Santa and Taft
31. Like a twang
32. Wrap
33. Confederate general, turned upside-down?
35. Modern plane
36. Peter, Paul & Mary: abbr.
38. Discourage
39. Rhyming trio
42. Edits
44. Gambler's advisor
46. Particular
47. Flightless bird
49. Sly looks
50. Annoying people
51. Cubicle
52. Hand lotion ingredient
53. First-rate
54. __ on; forwarded
55. Sweet snack item
56. __ , Nanette
57. Method: abbr.
60. __ Paulo, Brazil

1	2	3	4		5	6	7	8	9		10	11	12	13
14					15						16			
17					18						19			
20				21				22		23				
			24				25							
26	27	28				29				30		31	32	33
34					35				36					
37				38				39				40		
41			42				43				44			
45						46				47				
			48		49					50				
51	52	53						54				55	56	57
58					59		60				61			
62					63						64			
65					66						67			

ACROSS

1. Musical instruments
6. Sissy
10. Smell
14. 200 milligrams
15. Covers the cake
16. Silent performer
17. Queen's accessory
18. Law enforcers
20. David's son: abbr.
21. Secluded valley
23. Word with travel or insurance
24. Insects
25. Michael Learned's role on *The Waltons*
27. Period of time
30. Stack
31. Deborah Franklin's man
34. French pronoun
35. Naval detection apparatus
36. Flightless bird
37. Tried a serviceman
41. Primate
42. Littlest ones
43. Away from the wind
44. Directed
45. Miquelon et Réunion
46. Most popular tubers
48. __ so; extremely
49. Harbor bird
50. One lacking freedom
53. British dwelling
54. Item on a death certificate
57. Lunch spot
60. Veranda
62. __ *For All Seasons*
63. Spacious
64. Singer/pianist John
65. Ernie's buddy
66. Suffix for kitchen or luncheon
67. Complains violently

DOWN

1. Fall parts: abbr.
2. Scott of *Happy Days*
3. __ surgeon
4. Cob
5. Presented to an audience
6. Dries
7. Religious symbol
8. Allen or Gibson
9. With 10 Down, alphabetic conclusion
10. See 9 Down
11. Thinnest of six
12. Future indicator
13. Split
19. Tourist's item
22. Majors
24. Boxers Max or Buddy
25. Facilities in San Francisco and Fort Knox
26. Asia's__ Mountains
27. Transferable picture
28. Sneak away to be united
29. __ in; provided with the necessary information
30. Boston and New Orleans
31. Ball attendee
32. Mideast title: var.
33. Certain paintings
35. Less loony
38. Table top protector
39. Beast of burden
40. Past due
46. Refrain syllable
47. Caribou's feature
48. Happening
49. Bring joy to
50. Strikebreaker
51. Like a poor excuse
52. O'er yonder
53. Puncher's hand
54. Against: pref.
55. Spot for a Coventry con
56. Cologne numerals
58. Leading lady?
59. Plague carrier
61. Montgomery's place: abbr.

1	2	3	4	5		6	7	8	9		10	11	12	13
14						15					16			
17						18			19					
20				21	22					23				
			24					25	26					
27	28	29					30					31	32	33
34						35						36		
37				38	39						40			
41				42							43			
44				45					46	47				
			48					49						
50	51	52					53					54	55	56
57					58	59					60	61		
62					63						64			
65					66						67			

ACROSS

1. Late Huntley
5. One who "licked the platter clean"
10. Late coming back
14. Followers of fa or tra
15. Soldier's delight
16. Horse's feature
17. Greases
18. Devoured
19. Stain
20. Piece of furniture
22. Leftovers
24. Forest creature
25. Garden bloom
26. Gloria Bunker-Stivic's portrayer
29. Father of Robert, Edward, William and Tad
30. Semiprecious stone
34. "Woe is me!"
35. Snoop
36. Night noises
37. Loiter
38. Within __ ; not far away
40. Alphabetic characters
41. Reparation
43. Cut green blades
44. Lawsuit
45. Day
46. Piece of cloth
47. Resurrected
48. Palm tree
50. Earth tone
51. Beverage
54. Waltzing
58. Pause
59. Understood
61. Gardener
62. Yen
63. Beast of burden
64. "Old MacDonald had a farm, __ ..."
65. Greek letters
66. Conger seeker
67. Scum

DOWN

1. Clumsy one
2. Head covering
3. Magazine title
4. Parts of fezzes
5. Smooth and shiny
6. Fruit
7. Turncoat
8. Opposed
9. Creed article
10. Trade restriction
11. Bones
12. Shortly
13. "Why don't we!"
21. Deceitful
23. Intended
25. Immeasurably bad
26. __ dressing
27. 1836 battle site
28. Brewer's product
29. Departure's opp.
31. Regions
32. Uptight
33. German city
35. Breadwinners, often
36. Oinker
38. Ford
39. Glutton
42. Takes tiny bites
44. Made sure of: colloq.
46. Real estate transaction
47. Scurried
49. Official name
50. Ancient invader
51. Popular board game
52. Smart
53. Pond growth
54. Former phone call price
55. Ten cubed plus eleven
56. Poet's contraction
57. Stubborn courage
60. Destination in *The Grapes of Wrath:* abbr.

1	2	3	4		5	6	7	8	9		10	11	12	13
14					15						16			
17					18						19			
20				21				22		23				
			24				25							
26	27	28				29				30		31	32	33
34					35				36					
37				38				39				40		
41			42				43				44			
45						46				47				
			48		49				50					
51	52	53						54				55	56	57
58					59		60				61			
62					63						64			
65					66						67			

ACROSS

1. Shade tree
4. Rosters
9. Bustle
13. Dull thud
15. In the know
16. Sinister
17. Sightseeing trip
18. Female animals
19. Item on a birth certificate
20. Groups of descendants
22. Fermented substances
23. Breathe heavily
24. Suffix for Christ or Brazil
26. Preacher's spot
29. Cable TV station
34. Whirling
35. Item with 12 buttons
36. __ de plume
37. Gritty particles
38. Walter, Donna and Rex
39. Part of a ticket
40. __-pitch softball
41. Northern Europeans
42. Pronoun
43. Emerson or Lamb
45. More impoverished
46. Eisenhower or
    Schwarzkopf: abbr.
47. Go bad
48. Refuge
51. Dedicated
56. "Merrye __ England"
57. Recommendations for peo-
    ple with high cholesterol
58. College town
60. River in Africa
61. Identical
62. Scarce
63. Initials for Greer
64. Biblical weeds
65. Regulation

DOWN

1. Fitting
2. Make a mess
3. Little hand's indication
4. Sad song
5. Greedy child's words
6. Eastern garb
7. Magnolia
8. Meetings
9. Rent payer
10. Zero
11. Change on $3.00, when
    you buy 10 stamps
12. Aficionado's shouts
14. __ up; supported
21. Actor Max
25. Reverent fear
26. Old hat
27. Mount Narodnaya's
    range
28. Jay and family
29. Bed item
30. Coal scuttles
31. Bury
32. Quiet one
33. Glowing piece
35. Animal enclosures
38. Mac
39. Like February (compared
    with any other month)
41. Color transformer
42. Recommend highly
44. Concurs
45. Balances
47. __ detector
48. Pine
49. Tell __ ; prevaricate
50. Lounging around
52. Large-mouthed jar
53. Late Israeli prime minister
54. And others: abbr.
55. Woman's name
59. Original

PUZZLE 58

1	2	3			4	5	6	7	8		9	10	11	12
13			14		15						16			
17					18						19			
	20			21							22			
		23						24	25					
26	27	28					29	30				31	32	33
34					35						36			
37					38						39			
40				41						42				
43			44					45						
		46					47							
48	49	50			51	52	53					54	55	
56					57						58			59
60					61						62			
63					64							65		

ACROSS

1. Cotton-tipped item
5. Colorful bloom
10. Small progression
14. Carson's successor
15. River flowing through Paris
16. Prefix for prompter or vise
17. Countertenor
18. Punitive
19. Freedom from difficulty
20. Sore spot
22. Coal or phosphate
24. Not reversed
25. Paper appliqué
26. Baby bird's noise
29. Abbr. on an
    encyclopedia spine
30. Come together
34. Will name
35. *Diamond* __
36. Throw off track
37. As well as
38. Was relevant
40. Numerical prefix
41. Shows contempt
43. Word with American
    or purpose
44. Late Foxx
45. Danny Thomas' daughter
46. Craft made of gopherwood
47. Succinct
48. Collect
50. Prank
51. Evergreen trees
54. Encircled
58. "You don't know
    the half __ !"
59. Projection
61. Greedy person's desire
62. Places
63. French novelist Zola
64. "__ go bragh!"
65. Type of secretary: abbr.
66. Readjust
67. In good order

DOWN

1. Thick piece
2. Healthy
3. One opposed
4. Enthusiastic supporter
5. Poplar variety
6. Crystal ball gazer
7. Container
8. Part of a tooth
9. Keepsake
10. Pennsylvania athlete
11. Droplet
12. Ms. Maxwell
13. Part of an apple
21. Surpass
23. Called
25. Monetary units
26. Gap
27. Reddish tint
28. Sea duck
29. Bigwig, for short
31. Assessor
32. Surrounds
33. Slur over in pronunciation
35. Albums, for short
36. State: abbr.
38. Fragrance
39. Type
42. Waistband material
44. Regulated system
46. Take for granted
47. Part of a file folder
49. "... for spacious skies,
    for __ ..."
50. Say "hi" to
51. Tree trunk
52. Sly as __
53. Tiny insects
54. Leer
55. __ off; detached
56. Assam silkworm
57. Car scar
60. Fleur-de-__

PUZZLE 59

ACROSS
1. 144
6. Haul
10. Anger
14. Variety show
15. Projecting piece
16. In the manner of: It.
17. Concerning
18. Church response
19. Fictional king
20. Scary creatures
22. Painful emotional experience
24. Slimy swimmers
25. Alleged
26. Island ruler
29. Red foods
30. Shade
31. Dinner table article
33. Suit fabric
37. Sea eagles
39. Ham it up
41. Bellow
42. Evaluates
44. City in the Ruhr Valley
46. Sort
47. Discourage
49. Tease: colloq.
51. Economizes
54. Part of an old phone
55. Topics
56. Most hot-tempered
60. Left one's seat
61. Zest
63. Banishment
64. D __ David
65. Story
66. Warning sound
67. Proceeded
68. Tall pole
69. Playing cards

DOWN
1. Weight
2. __ , Nevada
3. Microwave
4. Daily phenomenon
5. Dogs
6. Sweethearts
7. Male animals
8. Street: abbr.
9. Tame
10. Sick feelings
11. Part of the small intestine
12. Part of a fire
13. Unit of capacitance
21. Unite secretly
23. Rising star
25. Change
26. Female superstar
27. Personal atmosphere
28. Dispatched
29. Lift
32. Portents
34. Insecticide
35. Shorebird
36. Ms. Sommer
38. Dregs
40. Start of a counting rhyme
43. Unchanged
45. Closest
48. Disturbs emotionally
50. Cure-all
51. Item served with a milkshake
52. Picked
53. Tree secretion
54. Traveler's stop
56. Refrain syllables
57. Emerald Isle
58. Weaver's reed
59. Dix and zehn
62. Track runner's distance

PUZZLE 60

ACROSS

1. Mariners' guides
6. Item in a desk drawer
10. Money specialists: abbr.
14. Interlaced
15. Former official name of a nation
16. Gymnast Korbut
17. Public building
18. __ Linda, California
19. Actual
20. Picture
22. Give
24. That femme
25. Removes
26. United
29. Cruise ship
30. Traveler's way: abbr.
31. Cars used by a dealer, familiarly
33. Partitions
37. Object
39. Respond
41. Expired
42. __ T
44. Nosy person
46. Fragrant accessory
47. Narratives
49. Enthusiastic
51. Those easily victimized
54. Czech river
55. Honey factory
56. Guiding sponsorship
60. Pain
61. Splinter group
63. "Stop!" on the seas
64. Skin scourge
65. Ending for Ann or Nan
66. French income
67. Rumanian coins
68. Raise
69. German city

DOWN

1. Switch
2. Bull
3. State with conviction
4. Leased
5. Was very unfriendly
6. Misrepresent
7. Major disturbance
8. Part of a river
9. Benumb
10. Got a monopoly on
11. Skirt feature
12. Hard stone
13. Realtor's delights
21. Rapidly growing tree
23. Spanish shouts
25. Nightclub
26. Part of a teacup
27. Chancellor __ von Bismarck
28. Requirement
29. Banking transactions
32. Level, raised areas
34. Stack
35. Ending for 7 numbers
36. Mine entrance
38. Answering machine's recordings
40. Amphibians
43. Den
45. Prime
48. Steamy spring
50. Uses a number 1 wood
51. Of a church leader
52. Quickly
53. Cheaply made
54. External
56. Judicial proceedings
57. Fires: slang
58. This: Sp.
59. Gun
62. Champagne season

PUZZLE
61

1	2	3	4	5		6	7	8	9		10	11	12	13
14						15					16			
17						18					19			
20					21				22	23				
			24					25						
26	27	28					29							
30				31		32				33		34	35	36
37			38		39				40		41			
42				43		44				45		46		
			47		48				49		50			
51	52	53					54							
55						56					57	58	59
60					61	62				63				
64					65					66				
67					68					69				

ACROSS
1. Fleur-de-__
4. Recede
7. Nothing more than
11. Tortellini
13. Successors of Popes
    Pius VII and Pius IX
15. Sahara-like
16. Story of a swan
19. Kingdome and
    Hoosier Dome
20. Planning skill
21. __ Thérèse of Lisieux
23. Digit
24. Catch sight of
27. Minute
30. Young Barrymore
34. Portion
36. Pharmacy purchases
38. Matador's encouragement
39. Most horrible
40. Abbr. in a bank's ad
41. Committed a crime
43. Nettle
44. Sultan's women
46. Subdued
47. Vegetarian's no-no
49. V-shaped rampart
51. Young and others
52. Part of a yr.
54. All __ ; ready
56. Oases for the thirsty
61. Göteborg residents
66. Novel with a WWI setting
68. Michigan, for one
69. Lose one's footing
70. Word with well or case
71. Vexed
72. Patriots' goals, for short
73. Cpl.'s superior

DOWN
1. Cowardly Lion's portrayer
2. Words of understanding
3. Shock
4. English isle
5. Places for roses
6. Struggle
7. __ milk
8. Tribal member
9. Marriage symbol
10. Not at ease
11. School carnival
    planning org.
12. Muslim officials
14. Torah
17. Nav. transports
18. Home for Dorothy
    and Aunt Em: abbr.
22. Kingdom
24. Coast
25. Jacket
26. Periods of time: abbr.
28. Made public
29. Mountain animals
31. Like a mansion
32. French pronouns
33. Unwanted growth
34. Sink's alternative
35. Afr. nation
37. Supersonic transport,
    familiarly
42. Part of the title of
    an X-O game
45. ← ↑ ←
48. __ and feathered
50. Egg container
53. Macabre author
55. Pairs
56. Indonesian island
57. Off in the distance
58. Dissolute man
59. Dissolve
60. Moved smoothly
62. Devours
63. Haul
64. Rising time
65. Division of a former
    nation: abbr.
67. 33s

PUZZLE
62

	1	2	3		4	5	6			7	8	9	10
11				12		13			14		15			
16					17					18				
19							20							
			21		22				23					
	24	25	26		27		28	29			30	31	32	33
34				35		36				37		38		
39						40				41	42			
43				44	45					46				
47			48		49				50		51			
		52	53				54		55				
56	57	58				59	60		61		62	63	64	65
66							67						
68				69					70			
71					72					73			

ACROSS

1. Most common first name for U. S. presidents
6. Ardor
10. Campus area
14. Remus or Sam
15. Common French verb
16. Biblical preposition
17. Clamor
18. Hit the ceiling
19. On
20. Imagine
22. City in Wisconsin
24. Lake birds
25. Singing group for Davy, Peter, Micky & Mike
26. Gathered
29. Strained vegetables
30. Bullring cry
31. Chopper
33. Fury
37. Animal with a snout
39. Leading
41. Ox's burden
42. Nursery rhyme Jack
44. City on the Rhone
46. Won back
47. Under __ ; confidential
49. Show affection for
51. Gifts from a crocheter
54. Whiten
55. Cup-shaped blooms
56. Rainy weather items
60. __ , Oklahoma
61. Have on
63. City northwest of Orlando
64. Sound
65. Suffix for kitchen or major
66. Certain paintings
67. Amphibians
68. Musical instrument
69. Common sites for trouser tears

DOWN

1. Beaver Cleaver's mom
2. Of unknown authorship: abbr.
3. VIII doubled times XXIII tripled
4. Women's names
5. Becomes enraged
6. Digits
7. Type of collar
8. Casa Mrs.
9. Great fright
10. Charlatan's claims
11. Loosen
12. Make reparation
13. Dummies
21. Second most populous country
23. Again
25. Wall covering
26. Crowds
27. Tilted
28. Scorch
29. Equals
32. Fellows
34. Excellent
35. Ref's decisions
36. Chops
38. Untanned skins
40. Appliquéd sticker
43. Pitfall
45. Bars
48. Piece of info given to a *Jeopardy* player
50. Save
51. Tête-__
52. Make __ ; ridicule
53. Flash
54. Reduced
56. Fence part
57. "Mary __ little lamb..."
58. Type of school: abbr.
59. Disrespect
62. Season for Mitterrand

1	2	3	4	5		6	7	8	9		10	11	12	13
14						15					16			
17						18					19			
20					21				22	23				
			24					25						
26	27	28					29							
30				31		32				33		34	35	36
37			38		39				40		41			
42				43		44				45		46		
			47		48				49		50			
51	52	53					54							
55						56						57	58	59
60					61	62				63				
64					65					66				
67					68					69				

ACROSS

1. Beach surface
5. Writing surface
10. Taj Mahal's site
14. Parts of small intestines
15. Composure
16. Word in an address
17. Particle
18. Football team member
19. Word with muscle or dial
20. Seasonal wind
22. News
24. Moose
25. Addicts
26. Old
29. Pilot's direction: abbr.
30. River mammal
34. Clothing
35. See 21 Down
36. Address
37. Sharp item
38. Finds repulsive
40. Single thickness
41. Colored
43. Charles, for one
44. Cowboys or Indians
45. Join
46. Marsh
47. Island whose capital
     is Canea
48. Receded
50. Mai __ ; cocktail
51. John the Baptist
     and John Fisher
54. Boils
58. Toward shelter
59. Crooked
61. Word with box or man
62. Zoom skyward
63. Like a corrupt official
64. Being: Lat.
65. Clothing edges
66. Talk to a crowd
67. Action

DOWN

1. Old name for a nation
2. Choir member
3. Bright light
4. Fairy tale misses
5. Ghost
6. Piece of meat
7. Feel miserable
8. Disease-carrying insect
9. Uncanny
10. Skilled person
11. Hired thug
12. "You __ ?"; Lurch's phrase
     on The Addams Family
13. Hot day drinks
21. Sound of support
23. Fumbles, in football
25. Escorted to a pew
26. New York, for one
27. Poison
28. Representative
29. Part of a wk.
31. Sioux shelter
32. Sparkle
33. Sound similar
35. __ Cross
36. Animals' home
38. Head topper
39. Most common word in
     California city names
42. Appears unsteady
44. Edged
46. Become ulcerated
47. Machine wheel
49. See 21 Down
50. Sir or Madam
51. Long-running TV show
52. __ vera
53. Enlarge an opening
54. Bench piece
55. Alleviate
56. Stand
57. Vehicle that spends much
     of its time being pulled
60. "__ pig's eye!"

1	2	3	4		5	6	7	8	9		10	11	12	13
14					15						16			
17					18						19			
20				21				22		23				
			24				25							
26	27	28				29				30		31	32	33
34					35				36					
37				38				39				40		
41			42				43				44			
45						46				47				
			48		49				50					
51	52	53					54				55	56	57	
58					59		60				61			
62					63						64			
65					66						67			

ACROSS
1. Crow
5. Pronto, in the office
9. Despised
14. Seldom seen
15. Padre, in Paris
16. Overact
17. River in England
18. Spread
19. Sophia
20. Northeastern resident
23. *Norma __* ; 1979 film
24. Light source
25. TV manufacturer
28. Journeys
32. Cavalry weapons
34. Furnace frame
35. Evict
37. State
38. Rajah's partner
39. Nitwits
40. __ , Nevada
41. One __ one is one
42. Brain passage
43. Noisy fight
44. Beautiful to view
46. Alfalfa, Spanky, et. al.
48. Rose's youngest
49. "Diamond State": abbr.
51. Australian bird
52. One who treats children
58. Marketplace
61. Kirghiz's __ Mountains
62. Birthplace for 19 Across
63. Wooden shoe
64. Thick cord
65. Once more
66. Slippery, sticky matter
67. Mlles. of Paradise
68. Works with leather

DOWN
1. Muffin ingredient
2. Talk wildly
3. Lined up
4. __ gap
5. Farthest point in an orbit
6. Exchange for cash
7. Carpet layer's
   calculation
8. Laborers
9. Capital city
10. Love: Sp.
11. Rocky hill
12. Part of the French year
13. Room
21. Parishioner's section
22. Does a
   household chore
25. Narrate again
26. Wading birds
27. "There was an old woman who lived in __ .."
28. Spell
29. Carried on
30. Ransack
31. Gas purchaser's choice
33. Governmental official
34. Mill grain
36. Poison remedies
39. Cut finely
43. Start of Theodore
   Roosevelt's presidency
45. Imagine
47. World __
50. Untrustworthy ones
52. School event
53. "Thanks __ !"
54. Record
55. Scottish island
56. Word indicating agreement
57. TV fare
58. Pompous fool
59. Qt. + qt. + qt. + qt.
60. Sash

PUZZLE
65

ACROSS
1. So. state
4. Totality
7. Red light's message
11. Smell
13. Laid back
15. One of the Three Bears
16. City southwest of Austin
19. Office employees
20. Agonies
21. Take into custody
23. Patriotic org.
24. Strange
27. Connect again
30. Quarrel
34. Gives off
36. Outer coatings
38. *You __ My Sunshine*
39. Not at ease
40. Connecting word
41. Advantage
43. Item on a
    death certificate
44. Sheen's opposite
46. Craft project purchase
47. Singing bird
49. Attack from all sides
51. Itsy-bitsy
52. Gardner
54. Noise
56. Type of cheese
61. Projecting pieces
66. City northwest of Albany
68. Use needles
69. Burn
70. Nickname for a man
    or a woman
71. In one's right mind
72. Altar constellation
73. Start of a U. S. capital

DOWN
1. Smell __ ;
   suspect trickery
2. Unaccompanied
3. To __ ; without exception
4. Fuss
5. Pocket residue
6. Den
7. Sharp objects
8. Vehicle
9. Ring stone
10. Achieve a C
11. Long-eared animal
12. Soon
14. Drunk: slang
17. Title no longer used
18. New Deal agcy.
22. Scold
24. Z's counterpart
25. Traveler's stop
26. Boozer's scourge
28. Does a beautician's job
29. Truly
31. No longer popular
32. Moutaineer's challenge
33. Head of France
34. Catchall abbr.
35. Part of a yr., at Yale
37. Fool
42. Observed
45. Early calculator
48. "Open hand": Japanese
50. Scrabble piece
53. Mr. Damone
55. Amphibian
56. Queries
57. Tropical starling
58. St. Brigid's land
59. Sailing
60. Close
62. __-in-the-wool; unchanging
63. Vampire movie element
64. Deviates
65. Pilot's milieu
67. Gun owner's org.

PUZZLE 66

	1	2	3			4	5	6				7	8	9	10
11				12		13			14		15				
16					17					18					
19							20								
			21		22			23							
	24	25	26		27		28	29			30	31	32	33	
34				35		36				37		38			
39						40				41	42				
43				44	45				46						
47			48		49			50		51					
		52	53				54		55						
56	57	58				59	60		61		62	63	64	65	
66							67								
68					69					70					
71						72					73				

ACROSS

1. Venetian blind piece
5. Jordanian
9. Night story
14. Invisible emanation
15. Wither
16. Spooky
17. In a __ ; huffy
18. Antitoxins
19. Source of wool, meat and milk
20. Capital
23. Reclined
24. Refrain syllable
25. Item for a Yankee
28. Locks
32. Suppose to be a fact
34. Gives up
35. Word of warning
37. Region
38. __ Major
39. Boat
40. __ Department; store section
41. Dye plant
42. Delete
43. Sun blocker
44. Like a foot & a yard
46. Insensitive
48. Distance driven ÷ amt. of gas used
49. Container
51. Letters of obligation
52. Place to buy rye
58. Church feature
61. Dryer fuzz
62. Famous bishop
63. Member of an Eastern religion
64. Freeway section
65. Algerian seaport
66. Rodent
67. Fly
68. Suffix for bald or bold

DOWN

1. Talk back
2. Moon: Sp.
3. Seed covering
4. Snitch
5. Analyzes ore
6. Use too much perfume
7. Swiss waterway
8. Brightly colored leaf
9. Burke and others
10. Depend
11. Period
12. Goal
13. __ culpa
21. Maiden
22. Fuming
25. FBI, for one
26. Reparation
27. Kid
28. Edible root
29. Moving upward
30. Dutch export
31. __ boom
33. Man for whom a large city is named
34. Misgiving
36. "...Christmas, when all through the house, __ ..."
39. Yellowish pink
43. Plum type
45. Fifth __
47. Mama dog's pride
50. Farms
52. Old-fashioned root beer
53. "Adieu, Giuseppe!"
54. Santa __ ; Mexican president of the 1800's
55. Word of assent
56. Greek letters
57. Sisters
58. Unit of electrical resistance
59. Atlantic resort, for short
60. Homonym for knew

PUZZLE 67

ACROSS
1. Caught some Z's
6. "Shoot!"
10. Wedge-shaped
    piece of wood
14. Modern medical device
15. "I cannot tell __ !"
16. Piece of glass
17. Bridal path
18. Bud holder
19. Fitzgerald
20. Bishops
22. Dug
24. Boys' school
25. Use up
26. 2 altos, 3 tenors
    and 2 baritones
29. Osmond
30. Flurry of activity
31. Wicked one
33. Part of a pie
37. Like some blackberries
39. Cook chopped onions
41. Word with crazy or fry
42. Impassive
44. Martin or Allen
46. Lemony concoction
47. Cut
49. Irritating skin sensations
51. Sacred cup
54. Suffix for mob or old
55. Luxembourg's location
56. Sudden outbursts
60. Among
61. December purchase
63. Variable stars
64. Half of a prison?
65. Worked on a birthday cake
66. On the ball
67. Do a lawn chore
68. Morris and Garfield
69. Complaints to a plumber

DOWN
1. Strike
2. Refuge
3. To be: Lat.
4. Tiny stone
5. Gave medical care to
6. Crow
7. "Ach!"
8. Poet's contraction
9. Sower's device
10. Bee entrants
11. Split down the middle
12. Stream
13. Union General
    George __
21. Bears
23. Narrative
25. One who attended Bo-
    logna University in 1287
26. Sharp tools
27. Make scholarly
    corrections
28. Outdoor sport
29. Dentist's view
32. Billiards stroke
34. St. George's place
35. Faction
36. Uno y uno y uno
38. Perform the
    Heimlich maneuver
40. Long-running
    Broadway play
43. Fastener
45. Endless
48. Containing vinegar
50. Like some New Orleanians
51. Desist
52. Weather word
53. Give someone __ ;
    phone
54. Snow toys
56. Extremities
57. Eye part
58. Ms. Overall
59. Beautician's offerings
62. Letters on some TVs

PUZZLE 68

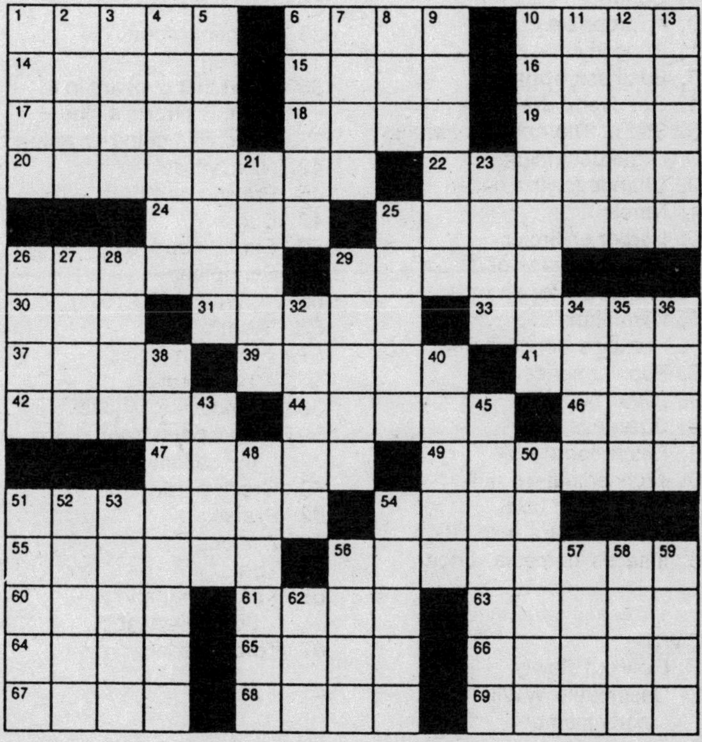
1
2
3
4
5
6
7
8
9
10
11
12
13
14
15
16
17
18
19
20
21
22
23
24
25
26
27
28
29
30
31
32
33
34
35
36
37
38
39
40
41
42
43
44
45
46
47
48
49
50
51
52
53
54
55
56
57
58
59
60
61
62
63
64
65
66
67
68
69

ACROSS

1. (8 x 8) − (9 x 7)
4. Capt.'s superior
7. Nuisance
11. Zooms aloft
13. Garlic's giveaway
15. Nabisco product
16. Nelsons
19. People
20. Candy bar
21. Approves
23. So: Scot.
24. Health club's offering
27. Coat fabric
30. Uncontrolled anger
34. Skunk's defense
36. British Parliament members
38. Word on every U. S. coin
39. Control
40. Appropriate
41. Bring joy to
43. Business abbr.
44. Get overly dramatic
46. Star of *The Addams Family*
47. Legal document
49. Change for the better
51. Nero's X
52. Harbor encircler
54. Take the place of
    another, for short
56. Olympians
61. Dentist's concerns
66. Popular series of
    the '60s
68. Soreness
69. Before long
70. Archaeologist's milieu
71. Freshwater fish
72. Natalie Cole's inspiration
73. Insect's nemesis, once

DOWN

1. Flow out slowly
2. Despicable WWII
   party member
3. Actress Moran
4. Labor Day: abbr.
5. Puts in
6. Luke-Acts connector
7. Hog
8. Indian tribe member
9. Mystical advisor
10. Preschoolers
11. Bawl
12. Dieter's lunch
14. Boosted
17. Questions
18. Letters on some TVs
22. Rarely
24. Setting
25. Goal of the United Nations
26. Reply: abbr.
28. Traveler's line
29. Lettuce and kale
31. Hard stone
32. Entered a car
33. Peaceful spot
34. Slipped
35. Word that appears in 6
    of this puzzle's clues
37. Word with going or sickness
42. Nav. vessel
45. Praying one?
48. Dug
50. Empty-headed
53. Sandpiper
55. __ War (1899-1902)
56. "Ach!"
57. Word with Texas
    or Georgia
58. Response to a joke
59. Note written from
    the bottom up
60. Greek portico
62. Praise
63. Zealous
64. Tore
65. Ken Griffey and
    Ed Begley: abbr.
67. Toronto's loc.

PUZZLE 69

ACROSS

1. Encyclopedias: abbr.
5. Puts two and two together
9. Talked & talked & talked
14. Lamb's pseudonym
15. Farmer's place?
16. Overdo the role
17. Requisite
18. Common verb
19. Put colored labels on
20. One with two pensions
23. Egypt, once: abbr.
24. Small amount
25. Place of rejuvenation
28. C, D, or AA
32. Desk drawer article
34. Mountain ridge
35. Freedom from stiffness
37. Voiced
38. Region: abbr.
39. Fine home
40. 0
41. Bridges
42. __ , Nevada
43. Eagle's feature
44. Cortez' victims
46. Walks
48. Word whose homonym ends in an *a*
49. Happy __ clam
51. Assam silkworm
52. TV profession for Bob Newhart before he became an innkeeper
58. Cleanser
61. __-up; car owner's expense
62. Unh-unh
63. Blazing
64. College in North Carolina
65. 21 Down, turned 90 degrees
66. Less stringent
67. Game piece
68. Great __

DOWN

1. Peddle
2. Product sold in cubes or tubs
3. Place
4. Unfortunate
5. Stick
6. No longer with us
7. CXXXIX quadrupled
8. Snoozed
9. Go back
10. Roman deity
11. Give the go-ahead
12. Suffix denoting origin
13. Sparks or Beatty
21. Overdue
22. Daily
25. Sacred parchment
26. Grands
27. Leader of the Green Mountain Boys
28. Wind
29. Provide with oxygen
30. Actual
31. Jerks
33. Like a neutral nation
34. Ready to swing
36. Chimney particles
39. Unkempt
43. Bull
45. Part of a swivel chair
47. Show mercy
50. Performed
52. Pierre, to his kids
53. Dance
54. __ about; approximately
55. Jot
56. Reach across
57. Prefix for type or scope
58. Presidential nickname
59. Son-gun connection
60. Recipe direction

PUZZLE
70

1	2	3	4		5	6	7	8		9	10	11	12	13
14					15					16				
17					18					19				
20				21					22					
			23					24				25	26	27
	28	29				30	31		32		33			
34						35		36			37			
38					39						40			
41					42					43				
44				45			46		47					
48				49		50			51					
			52				53	54				55	56	57
58	59	60				61					62			
63						64					65			
66						67					68			

ACROSS
1. Pronoun
4. 292 years before Columbus' famous voyage
7. Design
11. Embarks
13. Krung Thep resident
15. Cork County's location
16. Relocating
19. Offer as a plea
20. Cruelty
21. Today
23. Unit of heat: abbr.
24. Prefix for verb or noun
27. Of one's birth
30. Vehicle
34. Tropical vine
36. Direction indicators
38. Mr. Whitney
39. Homeric masterpiece
40. Letters for thousands
41. Lessen
43. Fellow
44. Distribute
46. Evil one
47. Kitty
49. Thing worth having
51. Feminine ending
52. Basker's desire
54. Cleaning item
56. Planner
61. Placed in a small recess
66. Remain committed
     to a position
68. Take care of
69. Scotch's accompaniment
70. Boundary
71. Without changes
72. Word with Red or White
73. Hallucinogen

DOWN
1. Paul, before he was Paul
2. Clarence Thomas'
    accuser
3. 1 Across, in French
4. Session: abbr.
5. Close friend
6. Outer garment
7. __ butter
8. Feel fondness towards
9. Greek god
10. Suffix for bold or cold
11. Place to rejuvenate
12. Indication
14. __ to; can
17. Type of light
18. Dynamite's cousin
22. Seesaws
24. Rice dish
25. Pours
26. Stop __ dime
28. Subdues
29. Pick up a ringing phone
31. Enlarges an opening
32. Singers
33. Manner
34. Drooping
35. Promotions
37. Blue
42. School event
45. Gliding dances
48. Positions
50. Fruity drink
53. Plus
55. Miss
56. Movie dog
57. Hwys.
58. Foreign princess
59. Son of Seth
60. Decorate again
62. Form a spiral
63. Makes music without
     voice or instrument
64. __ , Oklahoma
65. Dichlorodiphenyltri-
     chloroethane, familiarly
67. Woodwind

PUZZLE
71

ACROSS

1. Voyage
5. Leaflike part
10. Temporarily popular activities
14. Items made of nylon
15. Co-star for Hepburn
16. Hand lotion ingredient
17. "... forever and ever. __ ."
18. Change
19. Singer Vikki
20. Sophomoric
22. About 5, in London
24. Impersonate
25. Nightclub
26. Mantra
29. Final period: abbr.
30. Take to lunch
34. Force out
35. Prefix for meter or critical
36. Transfer to a third owner
37. Miscalculate
38. __ up; prepared to mount
40. Jimmy's follower
41. Conforms
43. Word with chicken or small
44. Remain unsettled
45. Riotous situation
46. Loiter
47. Ring stones
48. Means of transportation
50. Deface
51. Opposed to
54. Épée wielders
58. Monopoly game token
59. *Cheers* role
61. __ *Mary*
62. Highway path
63. Soup flavor
64. This: Sp.
65. 20 juin-to-21 septembre seasons
66. Uses a word processor
67. Intensely felt

DOWN

1. "... gave proof through the night __ ..."
2. St. Peter's locale
3. "¡Comprendo!"
4. Baseball team's goal
5. Actor's spot
6. Perry Mason's creator
7. Buchanan or Nixon
8. Like vinegar
9. Old strummables?
10. 2 and 3, to 6
11. __ Mountains
12. Student's room
13. Withered
21. To the point
23. Played a role
25. Expressionless one
26. Dairy product
27. Swarm of people
28. Of one of the senses
29. Palindromic verb
31. Like some seals
32. *Home __ ;* recent film
33. Looks after
35. Courtroom figures, for short
36. Reed
38. Like an unfriendly teacher
39. Record
42. Dresses for shorties
44. Thirsty
46. Long prayer
47. First page of a wall hanging: abbr.
49. Scarf
50. Ways' companion
51. Sufficiently skilled
52. Billy or Nanny
53. Superior
54. Word whose homonym ends in *w*
55. Freedom from pain
56. Church service
57. Insult
60. Napper

PUZZLE 72

1	2	3	4	■	5	6	7	8	9	■	10	11	12	13
14				■	15					■	16			
17				■	18					■	19			
20				21			■	22		23				
■	■	■	24			■	25					■	■	■
26	27	28			■	29			■	30		31	32	33
34				■	35			■	36					
37			■	38			■	39			■	40		
41			42			■	43		■	44				
45					■	46		■	47					
■	■	48		49			■	50				■	■	■
51	52	53			■	54			■	55	56	57	
58				■	59		60			■	61			
62				■	63			■	64			
65				■	66			■	67			

ACROSS

1. Hoover, for one
4. Cigarette substance
7. Poker risks
11. Very boring item?
13. Flower of Africa
15. Cream-filled cookie
16. 1965 Othello portrayer
19. Swindle
20. Like the most
    polluted room
21. Game for "it"
23. Desk item
24. Caesar
27. Switch
30. __ , Nevada
34. Less savage
36. Home
38. __ flash; suddenly
39. Enough
40. "...lead us __ into
    temptation..."
41. Intense beam
43. "Ghost" writer
44. Unclear
46. George and Barbara
    or Charles and Di
47. Stew ingredient
49. Numerical prefix
51. Numskull
52. Bustle
54. __-pitch softball
56. Stirred
61. Rubbed felt over slate
66. Plains man
68. Prefix for septic or trust
69. Use a knife
70. Hardware store purchases
71. Remainder
72. Albert, Ambrose and
    Anthony: abbr.
73. Fem. title

DOWN

1. Twofold
2. Malady
3. Nice mother
4. Part of the title of
   an X-O game
5. Beverages
6. Space
7. Cow
8. Tribe member
9. __ off; irritates
10. Type
11. Recent TV comedy
12. Geom. shape
14. United hastily
17. In order
18. WWII hero, for short
22. Farmers' group
24. Pago Pago's location
25. Push forward
26. Dover's place: abbr.
28. Nearly
29. Grandparents, often
31. Itemizations
32. Leg parts
33. Sails' alternatives
34. Bugle call
35. Final book: abbr.
37. Common street name
42. Battery size
45. Makes amends
48. Can't __ ;
    is unable to cope
50. Sir Guinness
53. Start of a state capital
55. Algerian port
56. Not shut
57. Lessen
58. Pts. and gals.
59. Chews and swallows
60. Word of disgust
62. Syria, once
63. Commotion
64. Sea denizens
65. Titles for Heathcliff Huxta-
    ble & Harry Weston: abbr.
67. Dieter's concern: abbr.

PUZZLE 73

ACROSS
1. Actress Gibbs
6. Filth
10. Card player's word
14. Other name
15. Noggin
16. Ms. Lee
17. Chanticleer's spot
18. God of war
19. Provo's neighbor
20. Orderly
22. Ingredient for soup,
    salad or sandwich
24. Name for a Cork lass
25. Gilbert or Manchester
26. Famous dog
29. Cottage cheese base
30. Toreador's
    encouragement
31. Perfume
33. Vehicle
37. Perplexed
39. Detection apparatus
41. Positive response
42. Avoid
44. Winds
46. Zeta's follower
47. Perfect
49. Trade
51. Becomes active
54. Mere's companion
55. Tell
56. Earmark
60. Smell __ ;
    suspect dishonesty
61. Site of a biblical
    wedding celebration
63. Nasal passages
64. Place
65. After that
66. Find out bit by bit
67. Pay attention to
68. Tools with teeth
69. Quench

DOWN
1. Prairie schoolteacher
2. __ vera
3. Noisy disturbance
4. Whips
5. Waldorf-__ Hotel
6. Columbus' burial place
7. Cleo's admirer
8. Native American
9. Experimenter
10. Oaths
11. Emanations
12. Editor's notations
13. Pacific island group
21. Tries to lose
23. Car manufacturer
25. Huge painting
26. Burden
27. Likewise
28. Part of a grapefruit
29. Waterway
32. Old robes
34. Song for The Judds
35. Mr. Johnson
36. By
38. Upset
40. Nonconformist
43. Revise copy
45. Malay garments
48. Puts up
50. Remember
51. Offensively bold
52. Weird
53. Writing surface
54. Arrangements
56. Over
57. Room size
58. Furniture wood
59. Slave
62. Cry of discovery

PUZZLE 74

1	2	3	4	5		6	7	8	9		10	11	12	13
14						15					16			
17						18					19			
20					21				22	23				
			24					25						
26	27	28					29							
30				31		32				33		34	35	36
37			38		39				40		41			
42				43		44				45		46		
			47		48				49		50			
51	52	53						54						
55						56					57	58	59	
60					61	62				63				
64					65					66				
67					68					69				

ACROSS

1. German exclamation
4. Actress Charlotte
7. Tower site
11. Green Mountain Boys' leader
13. Foot part
15. Parking valet tips
16. Abandon when in trouble
19. Least
20. Delta Sigma Theta or Alpha Kappa Alpha
21. Kassebaum or Metzenbaum: abbr.
23. Atomic __
24. Reserved
27. Award
30. Barriers
34. Unsmiling
36. Duncan
38. Site where one might pan for oro
39. Signed agreement
40. Strive
41. Calculating serpent?
43. Former Mideast alliance: abbr.
44. Cogs
46. Reclining
47. Icelandic literature
49. Insurance company investigator's finding
51. Cap & gown donners: abbr.
52. Lady Bird's follower
54. Misery
56. Happy family event
61. Slave of old
66. Fooling another
68. Fencer's prop
69. Elmer's product
70. Nervous
71. Old Olds
72. Automne's forerunner
73. Annual sports event: abbr.

DOWN

1. To __ ; precisely
2. Word with woman or coal
3. Hold
4. First name for a famous dog
5. Aardvark's lunch
6. Canyon sound
7. Rained cats and dogs
8. Pilate's inscription
9. Religious group
10. Pallid
11. Shade provider
12. Suffix for high or dry
14. Announce
17. News article
18. Ship's book
22. Mama bird
24. Place
25. Used one of the senses
26. Pts. of eras
28. Game pieces
29. No matter what else may be true
31. Enthusiasm
32. Manners
33. Miffed
34. Swing around
35. After expenses
37. Pay up
42. Salk and Sabin: abbr.
45. Corroding
48. Pie ingredients
50. Start of a Canadian province
53. Philippine native
55. Back __ ; New England, to Californians
56. Mimic
57. Trick
58. Substitute product
59. Flirt with
60. Of ships: abbr.
62. Staircase part
63. Duet
64. Handle: Lat.
65. Iacocca, for one
67. Tuition

PUZZLE
75

ACROSS

1. Makes a lap
5. Smelting refuse
9. Ring-shaped island
14. Entanglement
15. Sound of contentment
16. Did a farmer's job
17. Frankenstein's aide
18. This: Sp.
19. Linden and others
20. Fragrant shop
23. N. T. book
24. Masculine title
25. Montgomery's place: abbr.
28. Swears
32. Caught
34. Pancreas or thyroid
35. Sleep activities,
    for short
37. Word with hog or map
38. Frost
39. Small group
40. Tactless
41. Suffixes for salt or hero
42. Residents' endings
43. __ up; relaxed
44. Smaller
46. More offensive
48. WWII vessel
49. Time
51. Fall behind
52. Elation
58. In the know
61. Trip
62. One called "Terrible"
63. Parker's coin eater
64. Frolic
65. Longest river
66. Dinner dishes
67. Numerals
68. Delight

DOWN

1. Icy road danger
2. One who wrote *Bus Stop*
3. Implement
4. Severity
5. Harpoons
6. Overwhelming desire
7. Mr. Johnson
8. Picnickers' surface
9. Backward
10. Having mixed feelings
11. Homonym for a letter
12. Majors
13. Joseph Smith's
    religion, for short
21. Skirted student
22. Wimp
25. Stir up
26. Pioneer
27. Did arithmetic
28. Skirt styles
29. Easiest to handle
30. Run
31. Playing card
33. Charging in court
34. Barbecue
36. City in Arizona
39. Plant tendrils
43. Rising late
45. Conger fishermen
47. Drinks noisily
50. Houston slugger
52. Lager
53. In the near future
54. Show anger
55. Malicious
56. Bargain
57. Type of knife
58. Waking times, for short
59. Like a baby, often
60. Nourished oneself

1	2	3	4		5	6	7	8		9	10	11	12	13
14					15					16				
17					18					19				
20				21					22					
			23				24				25	26	27	
	28	29			30	31		32		33				
34					35		36			37				
38				39						40				
41				42					43					
44				45			46		47					
48				49		50			51					
			52				53	54			55	56	57	
58	59	60			61					62				
63					64					65				
66					67					68				

ACROSS

1. Exhausts
5. Dressing flavor
10. Vehicle for Princess Eugenie, once
14. Mouse's nemesis
15. Unite without fanfare
16. Irritate
17. Venetian dollar
18. Mississippi sights
20. Harem room
21. Native Americans
22. Architectural projections
23. Skinner
25. Add to so as to make sufficient
26. Buck
28. Reluctant
31. Dizzy
32. Stein contents
34. Suffix for self or Turk
36. Can't keep up
37. Sweetheart
38. In a different way
39. Samuel's teacher
40. __ well; is a good omen
41. Self-proclaimed expert
42. In short supply
44. Safe places
45. Juan's fishing spot
46. Cicero's first word, perhaps?
47. Like school paper
50. Continent: abbr.
51. Arachnid creation
54. Acts of penance
57. Diminish
58. Dangerous outpouring
59. Bespectacled character on TV's *Family Matters*
60. Hankering
61. "Ach!"
62. A, for a smart one
63. Lowly one

DOWN

1. French commune
2. Gobi-like
3. Handicapped one
4. Swirling bath
5. Napper
6. Change
7. Votes
8. Financial auditor: abbr.
9. Gown edge
10. Right
11. Inlets
12. Old man: Ger.
13. Disarray
19. Bush's Secretary of State
21. Russia's __ Mountains
24. Beverages
25. Word with for or which
26. Buttermilk's rider
27. Examinations
28. Grows gray
29. Chopsticks' alternative
30. German city
32. Mother __
33. Latin greeting
35. Layers
37. Nutty as a fruitcake
38. Jutting piece
40. Di, on 7/29/81
41. N. T. book
43. Sporting sites
44. Red tape
46. Silenced
47. Ooh-__
48. Eur. language
49. Variable star
50. Singer Paul
52. Therefore
53. Existed
55. Personal item kept at the office
56. Foul up
57. Young animal

1	2	3	4		5	6	7	8	9		10	11	12	13
14					15						16			
17					18				19					
20				21						22				
		23	24						25					
26	27						28					29	30	
31						32	33					34		35
36					37						38			
39				40						41				
	42		43						44					
		45					46							
47	48	49					50					51	52	53
54					55	56					57			
58					59						60			
61					62						63			

ACROSS

1. Title of respect
4. Dieter's platform
9. Biblical book
13. Jordanian
15. __ pole
16. Trot or gallop
17. Novel home
18. Came up
19. Pulitzer Prize-winning
    writer James
20. Smoother
22. Region: abbr.
23. Pickle
24. Have being
26. Put forth effort
29. Commission earner
34. Like a cliché
35. Residence, for short
36. Response to a preacher
37. Modern-day scourge
38. Robert and Elizabeth
39. Blood problem
40. Road danger
41. Do the lawn again
42. Loud sound
43. Makes insane
45. 737 and 747
46. Lincoln or Ford
47. Ballet and painting
48. Piece of wood
51. In a manner that
    lacks purpose
56. Hawaiian specialty
57. Herd
58. At __ ; relaxed
60. Mideast title
61. Shun restaurants
62. Crockpot contents
63. 62 Across ingredients,
    sometimes
64. University personnel
65. Poet's word

DOWN

1. Used a bench
2. Gershwin and others
3. __ avis
4. Rice, in China
5. Reef deposit
6. Preposition
7. __ majesty
8. May birthstones
9. Marbles
10. Pen
11. Part of a wedding cake
12. Suffix for rhyme
    or mob
14. Thieves
21. Maneuver for Spitz
25. Car of the past
26. Settled and steady
27. In a __ ; instantly
28. Passenger
29. Musical numbers
30. Over
31. Current location of da
    Vinci's *Last Supper*
32. Pedestal-ize
33. A-sharp and E-flat
35. Show up
38. Humiliated
39. Categories
41. Carrier of genetic info
42. Lunch orders
44. Oscar recipients
45. Primps
47. Famous chipmunk
48. Tread
49. Disabled
50. Cantata melody
52. Dies __
53. Former Dodger Manny
54. Lacking punctuality
55. River in Belgium
59. Homonym for a letter

1	2	3			4	5	6	7	8		9	10	11	12
13			14		15						16			
17					18						19			
	20			21							22			
		23						24	25					
26	27	28					29	30				31	32	33
34					35						36			
37					38						39			
40				41						42				
43			44					45						
		46				47								
48	49	50			51	52	53				54	55		
56					57						58			59
60					61						62			
63					64						65			

ACROSS

1. Chicken's sound
5. Unit of capacitance
10. Bridal veil material
14. Jai __
15. '60s skirt style
16. Part of President
    Arthur's name
17. Prehistoric home
18. Forbidden goods
20. Traveler's dir.
21. Buttonlike ornament
22. Musical symbols
23. Hairnet
25. Up to, for short
26. Like Astrodome games
28. Peaks
31. Stupid one
32. William Sydney Porter
    __ O. Henry
34. Grazing animal
36. Cosmetic producer
37. Grave sites
38. Aquino or Mubarak: abbr.
39. Siesta
40. Actress on TV's
    The Royal Family
41. Volumes
42. Real __
44. Rock salt
45. St.
46. Alexander's dueling foe
47. Lustrous fabric
50. Contraction
51. King topper
54. Constitutional changes
57. Hang around
58. Regal title
59. Numerical comparison
60. Descartes or Coty
61. Smell
62. Weather forecast
63. Quenchers

DOWN

1. Walk the floor
2. Spirited self-assurance
3. "Spies" with the ears
4. Pumpkin's destination
5. 2 or 7, to 14
6. Orally
7. Part of an orange
8. Crawling creature
9. German article
10. Tags
11. Lamentation
12. Hasn't the ability to
13. Purposes
19. One born between
    3/21 and 4/19
21. Before long
24. AM/PM divider
25. Singing syllables
26. "__ old cowhand from
    the Rio Grande..."
27. Variable stars
28. Refer to
29. Fired
30. Very pleasant
32. Away from the wind
33. Start of some Califor-
    nia city names
35. Being: Lat.
37. Rose
38. Sport
40. Was delirious
41. Bitter
43. Leather worker
44. Good-looking 19th-
    century carriage?
46. Moving
47. El __ , Texas
48. In the center of
49. Pianist Peter
50. One __ one is one
52. Wooden stick
53. Watches carefully
55. See 57 Down
56. Consume
57. Madrileña's title: abbr.

PUZZLE 79

1 2 3 4 5 6 7 8 9 10 11 12 13
14 15 16
17 18 19
20 21 22
23 24 25
26 27 28 29 30
31 32 33 34 35
36 37 38
39 40 41
42 43 44
45 46
47 48 49 50 51 52 53
54 55 56 57
58 59 60
61 62 63

ACROSS

1. Beast of burden
4. Stage items
9. Mr. Campbell
13. Kids
15. Hindu queen
16. Prefix for ballistics or nautical
17. Pennsylvania city
18. Lauder
19. Speak wildly
20. Carry
22. Sailing
23. Is located
24. Unsightly one
26. As a whole
29. Fragrant liqueur
34. Satellites
35. Eye movement
36. R & R
37. Noon-to-evening periods: abbr.
38. __ time; serving one's sentence
39. Olympic footgear
40. West
41. Old
42. Part
43. Honest
45. First name for a U. S. president
46. Word with Mexico or England
47. Pickle
48. Dictionary entry
51. Furthest from the center
56. Nostril titillater
57. Offer one's two-cents' worth
58. Religious painting
60. Heed one's alarm
61. Foolish admirer
62. Item on a birth certificate
63. Recognized
64. Haughty ones
65. Final book: abbr.

DOWN

1. Suffix for consider
   or compassion
2. Separate into categories
3. Recipe word
4. Pressure cooker name
5. Grates
6. Aware of the duplicity of
7. Equal
8. Furious
9. Mechanic's milieu
10. Pasturelands
11. Bird of the sea
12. __ bene
14. Falls
21. Tiny insects
25. Query
26. Muslim leaders
27. "Jack Sprat could eat __ ..."
28. Carrier
29. "...making __ and checking it twice..."
30. Playing card
31. Receiver
32. Instant
33. __ , Germany
35. Nonsense!
38. Sandwiches
39. Cut of meat
41. Bakery purchase
42. Coconut bearer
44. One of the Apostles
45. Electricians
47. Star in Cygnus
48. __ out; solve
49. Norse deity
50. Stood
52. Second word in a fairy tale
53. Late Communist leader
54. Skin mark
55. Book
59. Gambler's destination: abbr.

PUZZLE
80

1	2	3			4	5	6	7	8		9	10	11	12
13			14		15						16			
17					18						19			
	20			21							22			
			23						24	25				
26	27	28						29	30				31	32	33
34							35						36		
37						38						39			
40					41						42				
43			44						45						
			46					47						
48	49	50			51	52	53					54	55	
56					57						58			59
60					61						62			
63					64						65			

ACROSS
1. Ice formation
5. Large: pref.
10. First of zillions
14. Islamic nation
15. Pale
16. Ethnicity
17. Diplomacy
18. Deadlocks
20. Forest animal
21. Sea sight
22. Minds
23. Biblical outcast
25. Entire amount
26. Worshiped
28. Religious recitations
31. Stiff
32. Tugs
34. Second language taught
    in many countries: abbr.
36. Part of a balcony
37. Nonflowering plants
38. Graf __
39. Lyrical work
40. Type of rock
41. Edible mushroom
42. Magazine bigwig
44. Bundlers
45. Original
46. Grandma __
47. Diminish
50. Vast expanses
51. Weaken
54. Architects' papers
57. Lab dwellers
58. "...a real live nephew of
    my Uncle Sam, __ on..."
59. Go
60. High rating
61. State: Fr.
62. Recordings
63. Nonpareil

DOWN
1. Quote
2. __ Mountains
3. Swamped with
   unfilled orders
4. Suffix for persist
   or consist
5. Prepared spuds
6. Busy
7. Fellow
8. Episc. or Luth.
9. Word on a silver dollar
10. Like good farmland
11. Fruit
12. __-deucey
13. Difficult situation
19. Underground dwellers
21. Hastened
24. One of 5 "Greats"
25. Word with fine
    or liberal
26. Mr. Guthrie
27. Semiconductor device
28. Stick
29. Condition of the 1930s
30. Scornful look
32. Tolerate
33. Leftover
35. Becomes firm
37. Move smoothly
38. Food fish
40. Hard to scale
41. Bulk
43. Purpose
44. Crows
46. British unit of measure
47. __ Lane
48. Stain
49. Halo
50. Instant
52. Skin problem
53. House of Lords member
55. Alphabetic trio
56. Give __ go;
    make an attempt
57. Famous Chairman

PUZZLE 81

ACROSS

1. Large tree
4. Does penance
9. Sets
13. Gather
15. Bar, legally
16. Landed
17. Prefix for room or date
18. Horned animal, for short
19. Narrow way
20. Savior
22. Augury
23. Greek Orthodox artwork
24. Breather's need
26. Dreaded malady
29. Appeared nervous
34. Epic
35. Rare figurine
36. Nice friend
37. Secluded valley
38. Word with strip or book
39. OAS member
40. Govt. agcy. (1946-75)
41. City on the Rhone
42. Grand adjuster
43. Reuben-maker's need
45. Napoleon
46. Professionals' org.
47. Season
48. Summon
51. South Pacific islanders
56. Russian sea
57. Wed
58. Part
60. Dieter's drink
61. Showed again
62. Letter opener
63. Direction
64. Beverage containers
65. Soap ingredient

DOWN

1. Are reading up
2. Give for a time
3. Match
4. Zeal
5. Grayish
6. Prison: slang
7. Muscle quality
8. Irregular
9. In abundance
10. Ancient Persian kingdom
11. Hold the __ ; stand firm
12. British gun
14. Louisiana's state bird
21. Frosted
25. __ to Pieces Over You
26. Groucho's prop
27. Stray cat's milieu
28. Beatrice, to Di
29. Became very annoyed
30. Flower with 3 petals
31. Jeer at
32. Smoldering piece
33. Personal book
35. Vending machine
    purchase
38. Being
39. Creamy dessert
41. Location of the humerus
42. Foot-leg connectors
44. Item that is cast
45. Communion plates
47. Stringed instrument
48. Lawsuit
49. Locality
50. Fails to keep up
52. Over
53. Charter
54. Carol
55. Destroy violently
59. Poet's word

PUZZLE
82

ACROSS

1. Area __
5. Seaport in France
10. __ over; be forgotten
14. Male animal
15. Lofty abode
16. Bicycled
17. Mixed up
18. Bold outlaws
20. Group concerned with children: abbr.
21. Make eyes at
22. Keep from happening
23. Styles
25. In the past
26. Masseuse
28. Summits
31. Spiny-leafed plants
32. Frauds
34. __ Z; entire range
36. Command to Rover
37. Mariners' guides
38. Fratricide victim
39. College major
40. Exhausted
41. Beg
42. Declare
44. Pieces of wood
45. Word with body or way
46. Grieve
47. Liz's third and others
50. Money: slang
51. Relevant
54. Prince Charles, on 7/29/81
57. Parcel of land
58. *Call Me __ ;* Patty Duke's autobiography
59. Liqueur flavoring
60. Noisy impact
61. Study or kitchen
62. Like windows
63. Rope fiber

DOWN

1. Fellow
2. Hot spot
3. Ideal sweethearts
4. Ate up
5. Nag
6. Film holders
7. Gaelic
8. Taste of tea
9. Wooden peg
10. Accolades
11. Rich deposit
12. Stench
13. Start of the name of a U. S. state
19. Storms
21. Anthology entries
24. Submit
25. Weapons
26. Tabula __
27. Prefix for modern or violet
28. Transport
29. Cathedral feature
30. Place
32. Editor's notation
33. 3rd word of the National Anthem
35. Pioneer auto maker
37. Lively
38. Winglike
40. Meaning
41. Sulk
43. Tyrannical leader
44. Made a loud noise
46. Bullwinkle
47. Ski lift
48. Yes __ ?
49. Dean Martin's late son
50. Cut of meat
52. Baby carrier
53. Extra office helper
55. Opening
56. Ribonucleic acid, familiarly
57. Silvery-gray

PUZZLE 83

1	2	3	4		5	6	7	8	9		10	11	12	13
14					15						16			
17					18					19				
20					21						22			
		23	24						25					
26	27							28				29	30	
31						32	33					34		35
36					37						38			
39				40					41					
	42		43					44						
		45					46							
47	48	49				50						51	52	53
54					55	56					57			
58					59						60			
61					62						63			

ACROSS

1. Grad party planners
4. Dramatic division
7. Velvety growth
11. Blinds
13. Way of walking
15. Burden
16. Ultimatum
19. Program
20. Crown installers
21. State tree of
    Massachusetts
23. Western Indian
24. Rising times, for short
27. Intense beam
30. FDR's mom
34. Telegram words
36. Scatter
38. Pouter's "ridge"
39. Atoll encrustation
40. Sailor
41. Deteriorate
43. Santa __ , California
44. Final element
46. Place to eat
47. Zone
49. Don't exist
51. Eur. language
52. Four Monopoly board
    squares, for short
54. State: abbr.
56. Creamy desserts
61. Beach hut
66. Words addressed to
    the impatient
68. City on the Oka River
69. Waiter's item
70. Bakery purchase
71. Single
72. Fool
73. Came in first

DOWN

1. Smelting refuse
2. Gardener's tool
3. British gun
4. Past
5. King, for one
6. Floor piece
7. Oscar winners
8. Bills
9. Clubs
10. Vehicles for those
    in a hurry, for short
11. Bus depot: abbr.
12. __ with; support
14. Teacher's status
17. Over 7 feet
18. Siamese coin
22. Learn
24. Make amends
25. Ethical
26. Refreshing spot
28. Theater part
29. Short mission
31. Unattached
32. Equestrian
33. Impressionist
34. Wound covering
35. __-pitch softball
37. Get hitched
42. Equip
45. Bulldog, for Yale
48. Batter's delight
50. Word with Texas or Georgia
53. Rogers
55. Dial up
56. Fight decisions, familiarly
57. Of planes: pref.
58. Strip
59. Surrounding quality
60. Mantilla wearers: abbr.
62. Part of the face
63. __ time; never
64. Part of speech
65. Colony member
67. Method: abbr.

	1	2	3			4	5	6			7	8	9	10
11				12		13			14		15			
16					17					18				
19							20							
				21		22			23					
	24	25	26			27		28	29			30	31	32	33
34				35		36				37		38		
39						40				41	42			
43				44	45				46					
47			48		49			50		51				
		52	53				54		55					
56	57	58				59	60		61		62	63	64	65
66							67							
68					69					70				
71					72					73				

ACROSS

1. Perform
4. Plant pest
9. Borders
13. Lava
15. Ordinary language
16. Review another's manuscript
17. Father
18. Rings
19. Apportion
20. Confuses
22. Mare fare
23. Manner
24. Gobble
26. Breaks a commandment
29. Was amazed
34. Signs of things to come
35. Social division
36. Tumor: suff.
37. Let
38. Trails
39. Run
40. Have __ at; attempt
41. One of Disney's Dwarfs
42. Mediterranean cruise ship's stop
43. Mourned
45. Long-legged birds
46. Battery size
47. Fastener
48. Tarries
51. Attackers
56. "Wanna make __ ?"
57. Loyal servant
58. Force out
60. Playing card
61. __ in; join
62. Suffix for old or game
63. Hunter's prey
64. Theater necessities
65. Animal's home

DOWN

1. Cleo's downfall
2. Show approval
3. First aid kit item
4. Healthy snacks
5. Adorn oneself
6. Prank
7. Man, for one
8. Meal courses
9. Channel changer
10. Creative image
11. Sporting goods purchase
12. Geneviève et Clotilda: abbr.
14. Dress
21. Worst possible condition: slang
25. Address abbr.
26. Pretty color
27. Zee's counterpart
28. 1 Down's weapon
29. Paired
30. Wan
31. Italian-born actress
32. Ham it up
33. Social events
35. Headland
38. Drinks
39. Merchants
41. Chromosome material, for short
42. Rugged rock
44. Special Sunday
45. Bass holders
47. Narrow-minded one
48. Ground
49. Rose's lover, in play
50. Kelly
52. Feminine one, in Ulm
53. Antitoxins
54. Goes bad
55. Fat
59. Endeavor

PUZZLE
85

	1	2	3			4	5	6	7	8			9	10	11	12
13				14		15							16			
17						18							19			
	20				21								22			
			23						24	25						
26	27	28					29	30					31	32	33
34						35							36		
37					38							39			
40				41							42				
43			44						45						
			46					47							
48	49	50				51	52	53					54	55	
56						57						58			59
60						61						62			
63						64							65		

ACROSS

1. Crisp cookie
6. Night sight
10. Famous frontier gunfighter
14. "... an inch, and they'll take __ ..."
15. Pasture creatures
16. Autocrat
17. Student's concern
18. Military group
19. Versailles verb
20. Antenna
22. Concurs
24. Late coming back
25. Ring purchasers
26. Easy to slice
29. Prefix for bar or meter
30. "Camellia State": abbr.
31. Stopping place
33. One with a great burden
37. Meat choice
39. Goofy
41. Cry of pain
42. Trouser parts
44. Item on a check
46. Fellows
47. Largest organ
49. Enrages
51. __ the hills
54. Scottish language
55. Cleanses
56. Jones or O'Neill
60. Vehicle
61. Sightseeing trip
63. Like a gymnast
64. Staircase part
65. __ Anderson
66. Descartes and Coty
67. Pronoun
68. Symbol of servitude
69. Vertical

DOWN

1. Float on the wind
2. Confidante
3. Twain hero
4. Overjoyed
5. Like kin
6. Brain's protection
7. Slender, projecting part
8. Black cuckoo
9. Sale of goods directly to the consumer
10. Time after death
11. Montezuma, for one
12. Street show
13. Iron
21. "Who __ ?"
23. Party
25. In an appropriate way
26. Jabber
27. Verve
28. Item on a driver's license
29. Grinder
32. Plumbing parts
34. Green item
35. Impressionist
36. Upper house members: abbr.
38. Hotel employees
40. __ for; want badly
43. Faction
45. Catch
48. Extensively
50. __ counter
51. Shame
52. Cook onions
53. River animal
54. Inexplicable
56. Rubbish
57. Court-imposed penalty
58. Edison's field: abbr.
59. Relax
62. Three hugs

PUZZLE 86

1	2	3	4	5		6	7	8	9		10	11	12	13
14						15					16			
17						18					19			
20					21					22	23			
		24					25							
26	27	28				29								
30				31	32				33		34	35	36	
37			38		39			40		41				
42				43		44			45		46			
		47		48				49		50				
51	52	53				54								
55						56					57	58	59	
60					61	62			63					
64					65				66					
67					68				69					

ACROSS

1. Go by
5. Pops
9. Things to be learned?
14. Prefix for depressant or histamine
15. Esfahan's location
16. Not hidden
17. Meander
18. "See ya!"
19. AFL-CIO president (1955-79)
20. Post-Civil War profiteer
23. Vientiane resident
24. Mister
25. Address abbr.
28. Locks
32. Played in a lively way
34. Box
35. Barbie
37. Acted like
38. Make room changes
39. Saints' rings
40. Monster movie feature
41. 20th-century tyrant
42. Musical brothers
43. One who gets up
44. Lifts
46. Slumbered
48. Diploma hopefuls: abbr.
49. Pronoun
51. Furrow
52. Owner
58. *West Side Story* heroine
61. __ out; endured successfully
62. Marks for a whiz
63. Spoken
64. Word of agreement
65. Edge
66. Future, for one
67. Votes
68. Football players

DOWN

1. Recreational area: Fr.
2. Celebes ox
3. Bogart, to *Casablanca*
4. Fools
5. Marks of repetition
6. Middle Easterner
7. Facts
8. Obstacles
9. Cesar __
10. Four __ two is two
11. Small green item
12. Harbor soarer
13. Animal enclosure
21. At one's __ ; relaxed
22. Misses
25. Put side by side
26. Looked closely
27. Stranger
28. Quake
29. Boomboxes
30. Made up
31. Shoemaker
33. Official
34. Grouchy people
36. Suffer defeat
39. Must
43. Put to flight
45. Fiery speech
47. Is fussy about one's appearance
50. Bug killer
52. Pope __ XII (1939-58)
53. Birthplace for 52 Across
54. Notion
55. Be a breadwinner
56. Uttered
57. Houston and others
58. Porch item
59. Potable
60. Howard or Reagan

PUZZLE 87

ACROSS

1. Turf
4. Recommendations for sore muscles
8. Of the neighborhood
13. Aleutian island
14. Broncos' home: abbr.
15. Deteriorate
16. Complement
17. Of an age
18. Business transactions
19. Showy
22. Naval vessel, for short
23. Tried
24. Metric unit
26. Drifting
29. Goodies
32. Gemstones
36. Otherwise
38. U. S. writer James
39. In the center of
40. Witch's home
41. Restoration to health
42. Contemptible
43. Affirmatives
44. Unsmiling
45. Vending machine purchases
47. Actor's concern
49. Outbursts of laughter
51. Solution
56. *Ben* __
58. Top newspaper positions
61. Musical production
63. Give for a time
64. Altitude: abbr.
65. Flower parts
66. Ornamental trim
67. Cartoon roadrunner's word
68. Deputized group
69. European river
70. Beast of burden

DOWN

1. Take off
2. Web-footed swimmer
3. Because of
4. Panoramas
5. Red beverage
6. Jai __
7. Performs alone
8. Not as significant
9. __ pro nobis; pray for us
10. Business associate
11. Quenchers
12. For fear that
13. Electric guitar accessories, familiarly
20. Save up
21. Complete
25. Respond
27. Counter's start
28. Rapidly growing tree
30. Region: abbr.
31. Spotted
32. Pokes
33. Amo, amas, __
34. Differs in opinion
35. Swell situation?
37. Unexceptional
40. Let up
44. Elected ones: abbr.
46. Satisfy
48. Place for stored food
50. Foolish
52. Biblical queen's home
53. Stratagems
54. Swords
55. Common French abbr.
56. Place with many beds: abbr.
57. Until
59. Social affairs
60. In the past
62. House divs.

	1	2	3		4	5	6	7		8	9	10	11	12
13					14					15				
16					17					18				
19				20				21		22			
23							24		25				
				26		27	28		29			30	31
32	33	34	35			36		37		38			
39					40					41			
42				43				44				
45			46			47		48				
	49				50		51		52	53	54	55
56	57			58			59	60				
61		62			63				64			
65					66				67			
68					69				70			

ACROSS
1. Lunch for señor
5. Tutuila's location
10. Friends who use francs
14. Bird's feature
15. Oak nut
16. Baseball's Blue
17. Drinks liqueur
18. Deficiencies
20. Luau offering
21. Got rid of
22. Tees off
23. LP alternatives
25. Ointment
26. Subject of the Emancipation Proclamation
28. At once
31. Whitened
32. Yellow-billed birds
34. Tree
36. Kuwaiti leader
37. Tear to pieces
38. Spartan queen
39. Common verb
40. Like a chimney sweep's clothes
41. Places
42. Waterway
44. Bottom surfaces
45. __ over; finished
46. Don't exist
47. Struck
50. Be acquainted with
51. Bit of residue
54. Overabundance
57. Muffin topper
58. Cookie
59. Impressionist painter
60. In good health
61. Shorebird
62. Building level
63. __ Stanley Gardner

DOWN
1. Recipe abbr.
2. First four of five
3. Wealthy businessman
4. Approves
5. Accessories
6. Flu symptoms
7. Happiness or depression
8. Boston Bruin Bobby
9. Crawling critter
10. __ oneself of; uses
11. Factory
12. Lounging around
13. Brat's response
19. Lets go
21. Ran
24. Declare to be true
25. Taft, to Yale, for short
26. Gush forth
27. Religious men
28. Victim
29. One who is dry
30. More ancient
32. Injection
33. Scrap
35. Church ceremony
37. Earth
38. Leo
40. Auctions
41. Committed homicide
43. Fixed portion
44. Snowman's name
46. Goose genus
47. Opening
48. Female animal
49. Atop
50. Game of chance
52. Broker's advice
53. Golfer's target
55. Ship letters
56. Have-__ ; underprivileged one
57. Homonym for a letter

1	2	3	4		5	6	7	8	9		10	11	12	13
14					15						16			
17					18				19					
20				21					22					
		23	24					25						
26	27						28				29	30		
31					32	33				34			35
36				37					38				
39			40					41					
	42		43				44						
	45				46								
47	48	49			50				51	52	53		
54				55	56				57				
58				59					60				
61				62					63				

PUZZLE 1

```
S T R A P ■ T O O T ■ T O O L
P R A T E ■ A M A H ■ R U B E
E A S E L ■ C A F E T E R I A
E M P ■ L A I R ■ ■ E A S E D
■ ■ P E R T ■ C O E D ■ ■ ■
D O N A T E ■ C H A P ■ S S S
O M I T ■ ■ S A U T E ■ T O A
P E T E R A N D T H E W O L F
E N E ■ A D O R E ■ ■ H O V E
S S R ■ P E R E ■ G U I D E S
■ ■ L I N T ■ S E N T ■ ■ ■
A R T I E ■ ■ I T L L ■ C O D
C A R T R I D G E ■ A G O R A
T I E R ■ S O O N ■ C O V E T
I D E E ■ H E R O ■ E D E M A
```

PUZZLE 2

```
■ S H E ■ C R A B ■ L O G A N
P T A S ■ H A L E ■ E R O D E
E R I S ■ A S T A ■ S O L I D
W A T E R S P O R T S ■ D T S
S P I N E T ■ ■ S E E D S ■
■ ■ ■ D E C A ■ A R O M A S
L A D D S ■ A W E S ■ M I C E
O T O E ■ P L A C E ■ E T R E
F O W L ■ E M I R ■ A S H E N
T E N T E D ■ T U R N ■ ■ ■
■ G A L A S ■ ■ U T A H A N
A P R ■ A L P H A B E T I Z E
L E A S T ■ R A U L ■ O N U S
O L D I E ■ E I R E ■ M E R S
T E E N S ■ E R A S ■ S S E
```

PUZZLE 3

```
S P A T S █ R E E D █ R I M S
C A R E T █ A C M E █ A R I A
A L T A R █ T H U M B T A C K
R E S █ O L E O █ █ R E N E E
█ █ █ E K E D █ A B E L █ █ █
C R A V E D █ A L E A █ S T S
A I D E █ A B O R T █ T R I █
S C A R B O R O U G H F A I R
T E G █ A M E N D █ A N T E █
E R E █ K A N E █ W A R D E N
█ █ █ P E R T █ P A G E █ █ █
S A V E R █ S O R E █ A L I █
T R A N S M I T S █ N O T E D
L A N D █ A L E E █ T R O V E
O L E S █ P E T S █ S E P I A
```

PUZZLE 4

```
E G G S █ A R R A S █ M A M A
S H I P █ L O O S E █ A P O D
T I L E █ P L A T A █ R E N E
█ J A C K I E R O B I N S O N
█ █ I N N S █ █ O N E █ █ █ █
C O F F E E █ D I A G R A M S
A L L I E █ M O O R E █ B E T
B L O C █ R O U N D █ B E L A
A I R █ S A L S A █ R A T E L
L E A S A B L E █ P A S S E L
█ █ O R B █ █ D I N T █ █ █ █
B I L L I E J E A N K I N G █
A C I D █ T A S T E █ N E L L
S E R E █ E N T E R █ G A E L
E D E R █ D E E D S █ S L E D
```

PUZZLE 5

```
  C A N   S E R E   P E A C E
U R G E   T R I P   R A G E D
M E O W   R I S E   A T R I A
P E R S N I C K E T Y   E L M
S P A Y E D     S I E G E
      S E A T   A R O M A S
S I G H T   R E A R   R E N T
O G R E   M A N N A   E N C E
F O U L   A L E E   A S T E R
A R M L E T   T W I T
  B O N E R     D E A D L Y
L I L   C R E S C E N D O E S
E L E N A   S A R A   A N N E
S I R E S   E V E L   M U I R
T A S T E   T E E S   S T N
```

PUZZLE 6

```
G R A Y   M E T A L   D A R T
R O P E   A B A S E   O L I O
A M P S   S O U P T O N U T S
D E L   C O N S     D U M A S
    I R O N Y     T O T
S T A I R S   C U R S E S
P E N C E   P L A N S   L O T
O N C E   N A I V E   D A L I
T E E   S O L V E   C A B I N
  T S E T S E     P A R O D Y
    L E E     A L T E R
S T E E R   P T A S   A N D
C O N C E S S I O N   S T I R
A D I T   A P P L E   R E L Y
R O D S   G A E L S   A D E S
```

PUZZLE 7

```
L A B   S H A M   D E B A R
P A R A   H A L E   A R E N A
I B I S   A L A D   H A D E S
T E S T I M O N I A L   S T E
S L E E V E     C R I S P
      A D I T   L A U R E L
H E M A N   D O P E   P E L E
E V E L   C L U E S   E A S E
L E D A   A E R O   O R D E R
P R I M E D   S N A G
    C O D E R     S L O P E D
A G A   S T O R Y T E L L E R
B U T T E   O I S E   D A R E
C R E E L   S T E R   E N I D
D U D E S   T E R N   N E E
```

PUZZLE 8

```
P A C T   P A I N T   C A S H
A U R A   E S T E E   A L O E
S T O P   S P E E D T R A P S
S O S   S T E M   A M I S S
    S H E E N   D I E
C A R E E R     B A N N E R
R O O M S   T R A I T   D O T
E R A S   L A I R S   A S S E
E T D   H E R O D   B R U I N
    A S S E S S   S O I L E D
      T A T   P E N A L
C R E E P   B A N E   I R A
H O M E S T E A D S   O V E R
E M I R   A F I R E   W A N E
R A T S   E T T E S   E N D S
```

PUZZLE 9

PUZZLE 10

PUZZLE 11

```
A L A S   M A R D I   D A D A
C A R E   A G A I N   E L A N
T I E R   D I V E S   A U T O
  D A V I D L E T T E R M A N
    A L E E     R A T
O P E N E R   S L U S H I E R
P A S T A   E L E C T   S L O
T U T S   A R E N T   C L I O
I S E   E G R E T   S L E D S
C E R A M I S T   C L O S E T
    G I T     S E A S
A N G E L A L A N S B U R Y
C O R N   T O R O S   R O E S
N U I T   O N I O N   E T A S
E N D S   R I A T A   S E R E
```

PUZZLE 12

```
A N D E S   S P O T   A T T U
C A R A T   H E A R   D O E S
T I A R A   I N F A T U A T E
S L Y   B L E D   E L D E R
    S L E D   T R E T
B A L L E T   R O A M   B E G
E L E E   A E R I E   E L L
R E D W H I T E A N D B L U E
E R G   A B A S H   A I D A
A T E   R I L E   C A R E E N
    B A S E   W A R E
I O T A S   M A R T   F R Y
B L O S S O M E D   I D E A S
A I R S   L A T E   S U R G E
R O T O   D E E R   T O N E R
```

PUZZLE 13

PUZZLE 14

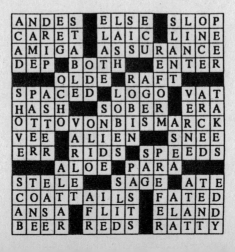

PUZZLE 15

PUZZLE 16

PUZZLE 17

```
S W A P . M A L T S . S A C K
C O L O . A R E A L . T M A N
I R A S . S C A L E . R E N O
. K I T C H E N C A B I N E T
. . C O E D . . Z I P . . . .
S T R A P S . E M I N E N C E
T H E R E . F L O E S . O H S
R A I D . C O L O R . P L A N
A N N . J O N E S . C R A N E
D E S C E N D S . C L I N T S
. . . L E T . M A I M . . . .
L I F E P R E S E R V E R S .
O K L A . A L E N E . V I L E
M E A T . C L A S S . A L A N
A S K S . T A T A S . L E G S
```

PUZZLE 18

```
A T E A M . S L A P . T H A R
B R A C E . T I R E . R U L E
C O S T A . R E T R A I N E D
D Y E . G O O D . . C A G E S
. . H E L P . S L E D . . . .
A S S U R E . S O O T . S O B
R O L L . E N N U I . L I I
G R E A T G R A N D C H I L D
U T E . B A R R Y . I D E E
E S P . O T O E . A S T E R N
. . O N E R . C U T S . . .
C R A V E . P A G E . L A W
H O M E S T E A D . E R A S E
A V E R . E D G E . L I N E D
P E N T . C O O T . S O D A S
```

PUZZLE 19

B	L	A	H		S	P	A				A	W	E	S
L	E	T	I		C	O	N	G	A		L	I	V	E
O	N	O	R		O	R	D	E	R		I	D	E	A
C	O	M	E	T	O	T	E	R	M	S		E	R	R
		S	A	T		S	M	I	L	E	S			
S	A	P		P	E	A		S	N	A	P	P	E	R
T	R	A	V	E	R	S	E			B	O	R	N	E
O	I	S	E		S	A	T	E	D		C	E	D	E
A	S	T	E	R			O	V	E	R	H	A	U	L
T	E	E	P	E	E	S		A	B	A		D	E	S
		U	S	A	G	E	S		A	N	A			
F	A	R		D	R	A	M	A	T	I	Z	I	N	G
A	T	I	E		E	T	U	D	E		U	R	A	L
D	O	Z	E		T	O	T	E	R		R	A	R	E
E	P	E	E			S	S	S			E	N	C	E

PUZZLE 20

A	D	D			T	A	M	P	A		H	A	R	D
P	E	A	R		I	D	I	O	M		A	B	E	E
T	A	M	E		S	U	N	U	P		N	I	N	E
	L	E	G	I	S	L	A	T	E		S	T	O	P
		R	O	U	T			R	E	O				
D	E	L	E	T	E		S	T	A	M	M	E	R	S
A	N	I	T	A		S	I	E	G	E		V	A	T
T	U	N	S		T	O	R	T	E		R	I	T	A
E	R	E		P	U	R	E	E		T	A	C	I	T
S	E	R	R	A	T	E	D		D	I	T	T	O	S
		O	D	E			P	A	N	T				
S	C	O	T		L	A	T	E	R	A	L	L	Y	
H	O	R	A		A	G	E	N	T		E	A	S	T
A	T	A	T		G	R	A	C	E		R	U	E	D
D	E	L	E		E	A	S	E	D		D	R	S	

PUZZLE 21

P	O	M	P		A	M	A			S	T	E	P
A	M	E	R		G	I	R	T	S		A	R	L	O
N	A	S	A		I	N	S	E	T		P	A	L	E
T	R	A	D	I	T	I	O	N	A	L		N	E	T
		O	D	A		N	O	V	E	L	S		
A	N	I		O	T	E		R	E	N	E	G	E	S
M	I	N	D	L	E	S	S			S	A	R	A	N
I	N	F	O		S	T	E	L	A		P	E	S	O
S	T	O	R	M			E	M	B	O	S	S	E	R
S	H	R	I	M	P	S		N	O	W		S	S	E
	M	A	D	R	A	S		U	N	A			
R	C	A		C	O	M	P	E	N	S	A	T	E	D
O	L	L	A		W	O	U	L	D		R	I	S	E
C	U	L	L		L	A	D	L	E		O	M	A	N
K	E	Y	S			S	A	D		N	E	U	T	

PUZZLE 22

S	C	O	F	F		L	I	V	E		S	T	U	B
C	O	C	O	A		O	R	A	L		P	A	S	O
A	L	T	E	R		V	A	L	I	D	A	T	E	D
M	A	O		M	I	E	N		E	R	A	S	E	
		H	E	R	D		H	A	T	E				
B	E	W	A	R	E		L	O	B	E		E	N	G
O	V	A	L		T	A	M	E	S		G	O	O	
G	E	T	S	T	H	E	B	E	T	T	E	R	O	F
U	R	E		R	I	P	E	R		R	E	N	O	
S	Y	R		A	R	I	L		C	R	A	T	E	R
		I	C	E	D		T	A	I	L				
E	V	A	D	E		G	I	L	T		A	W	E	
D	A	R	E	D	E	V	I	L		U	L	C	E	R
A	L	T	A		S	A	L	E		A	I	M	E	R
M	E	S	S		P	T	A	S		L	E	E	D	S

PUZZLE 23

PUZZLE 24

PUZZLE 25

```
O B I   H A M E S   C R O W
V O L T   A B I D E   L O V E
A S I A   R U D E R   A M E N
  C A V O R T I N G   R E N T
    E G I S     E W E
A D O R E S   T R A I T O R S
C R A N E   S U I N G   R O T
R A T S   R O B O T   C A M E
E K E   B E R E T   F I N E R
S E R V I C E S   C A N T O N
    I D I     S A R D
S L I P   T E M P T R E S S
L A D E   A V I A N   R I T E
I C E R   L I N D A   S L E D
M E S S   S L E E P     O W S
```

PUZZLE 26

```
C R A B   M A D     O G R E
H E M O   A B Y S M   F R E D
I D E A   N I E C E   T U N E
C O N S I D E R A T E   B E N
    T R A   S P E A R S
A L S   E T A   E S T A T E S
D E C A D E N T     S T A V E
O V A L   S T U B S   E K E D
P E R O N   G A N G R E N E
T E E N E R S   D I E   S S R
    C E R E A L   V A T
A P R   D E L I B E R A T E D
B O O T   L E V E L   P A R A
L O W S   S M I T E   E M I R
E L S E     D A D   R E E K
```

PUZZLE 27

PUZZLE 28

PUZZLE 29

S	H	I	R	T		S	T	A	R		C	P	A	S
E	A	G	E	R		H	E	R	O		R	A	S	P
E	L	O	P	E		E	A	T	S		E	S	T	A
S	T	R	A	N	G	E	R		T	E	A	S	E	R
		S	T	O	P		B	E	R	S	E	R	K	
C	A	S	T	O	R		P	A	R	S	E			
A	B	E		N	E	V	E	R		T	R	A	D	E
R	E	A	D		S	E	N	O	R		S	L	A	P
E	L	M	E	R		N	A	N	A	S		A	R	E
		M	O	G	U	L		P	E	T	I	T	E	
C	R	E	A	T	E	S		D	E	L	E			
R	U	N	N	E	R		C	A	D	E	N	C	E	S
A	P	O	D		M	A	U	L		C	U	O	M	O
P	E	L	E		A	C	R	E		T	R	A	I	N
S	E	A	R		N	E	S	S		S	E	L	L	S

PUZZLE 30

A	C	R	E	S		S	P	A	N		C	A	S	A
C	R	E	P	E		T	A	P	E		L	E	E	S
T	O	N	I	C		O	D	E	R		U	R	N	S
S	W	E	L	T	E	R	S		V	I	S	I	O	N
		O	I	N	K		L	E	S	T	E	R	S	
T	A	N	G	O	S		A	I	S	L	E			
A	L	A		N	U	R	S	E		E	R	A	S	E
L	I	V	E		E	A	T	U	P		S	L	A	G
K	E	E	P	S		T	O	T	A	L		O	N	A
		A	I	L	E	R		S	E	A	T	E	D	
S	H	O	U	T	E	D		E	T	A	L			
H	A	I	L	E	D		G	R	A	F	T	A	G	E
I	D	L	E		G	E	A	R		A	A	R	O	N
M	E	E	T		E	R	G	O		G	R	U	N	T
S	S	R	S		R	E	A	R		E	S	T	E	E

PUZZLE 31

```
A P E   M A D A M   S P A N
M A T H   A G A T E   P A L E
I N R E   N O N O S   R I O T
  T E L E G R A P H   I D E S
    P L E A     W I T
C A R E E R   B O O K E N D S
A L A R M   B L A R E   A I T
M O P S   F L A S K   M I C A
P H I   D A U N T   S A V E R
S A D D E N E D   C A G E R S
    R E F     B U R N
H O P E   A Q U A R I U M S
A S I A   R U S S E   M A L T
S L U M   E I D E R   S C A R
H O S S   S P A R S   S P Y
```

PUZZLE 32

```
M A D A M   W H I M   P A R D
A L A M O   H O N E   A C U E
L A T I N   I S N T   W I P E
T R A N S A C T   T E N D E R
    U T A H   G L A S S E S
C H A S E R   F R E S H
H U B   R O G U E   T O G A S
A L E S   N A M E D   P A L E
P A T E R   T E N E T   N E E
    E I D E R   M E R G E R
C R A D L E D   N O A H
O O D L E S   D E N T I S T S
R U D E   E D I E   I N L E T
E T E S   R U E D   M O O L A
R E D S   T E D S   E S T E R
```

PUZZLE 33

PUZZLE 34

PUZZLE 35

```
R A P T ■ C R O P ■ C A R O L
O M A R E ■ R O D E A ■ A L O N E
M I R E ■ A V O N ■ N O T E D
P E R S E V E R A N C E
■ P I E ■ L I E ■ A B E
■ H E A R S A Y ■ T R A V E L
P A R S E ■ R A V E ■ D E A L
A L A S ■ L I N E R ■ A R T E
L O S E ■ O A K S ■ A P S E S
S E E S A W ■ S T A R T E R
Y D S ■ V E E ■ B E A
■ P E R P E T U A T I N G
J A P A N ■ I T E S ■ I D E A
O W I N G ■ C R E E ■ O L I O
T E N S E ■ S E N D ■ N E L L
```

PUZZLE 36

```
C O L I C ■ A B B E ■ S I K H
A R E N A ■ B O A R ■ C L E O
L E A S T ■ A U R A ■ A L A N
F O R E C A S T ■ S O L A C E
■ R A R E ■ H E A L T H Y
B A T T L E ■ P E D R O
A L I ■ L E P E R ■ S P E A R
N E E D ■ L E D O N ■ S A T E
E S S E S ■ S A N E R ■ S E A
■ C A R O L ■ P E S T E R
D A M A G E S ■ T A L E
A B I D E S ■ V A L A N C E S
R O T E ■ A C E S ■ T O R A H
T U R N ■ L U S T ■ E R O S E
S T E T ■ E T T E ■ S A W E D
```

PUZZLE 37

PUZZLE 38

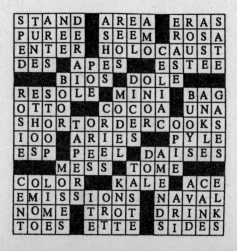

PUZZLE 39

```
    T L C     H A M     C U E R
A R I A S   A S I A   O P I E
M A K I N G T H E B E S T O F
O P E N E R   E N O R M O U S
        E A R     U N O
  L A P   D E M O N   S C A M
L O V E R   H A R D Y   R N A
A R E T E   I N D   A G E N T
M A R   P A R S E   M U S E S
A N T S   P E E R S   M T S
    E T A     S Y R
A B S E N T I A   S A T I R E
G E T S T H E B E T T E R O F
E L L A   Y S E R   S T O U T
S T O W     T S E   E N T
```

PUZZLE 40

```
L O A D   A B B E   A L I A S
A N N E   B O O M   F O R G E
S O D A   R O L E   L O S E R
T R I C K O R T R E A T
    T I A     Y A M   A T E
  G R I N D E R   G E R M A N
S L A V E   V I L E   O A S T
P I C A   C E D A R   A N T E
A D I T   A R E S   A D D E R
R E S E N T   R H U M B A S
E S T   O E R     N I L
    F O R E S H A D O W E D
A C T E D   S L A B   C A R E
M O R E L   T I L L   K I L N
S N I D E   S M E E   S T E T
```

PUZZLE 41

PUZZLE 42

PUZZLE 43

```
B A L D   P R O W S   R A P T
A L O E   L I C I T   E R I E
L I O N   A S T R O   G A T E
L E T T U C E   I M P A L A S
    I S E   S N A I L     L
E R A S E   R I G   L E G A L
D I R T   A I T   R E D E A L
A V E   A B D U C T S   N R A
M E N A C E   A R E   D O O M
S T A R T   S T Y   D I A N A
    M I N C E   B O A
R E C O V E R   D I S P O S E
O D O R   S E V E R   E V E R
W I N E   T A I N T   R A M S
S E E D   S M I T H   S L I T
```

PUZZLE 44

```
  G A P   I M P     T A B U
A I R E D   S A L A   A B A T
B R I T I S H C O L U M B I A
E L D E R S   E Y E T E E T H
    E T A     R E S
  T A B   S L A N T   T R O T
R E C U R   B R E S T   A V E
E M O T E   I C E   O D D E R
A P R   C A N E D   Y E A R N
L O N G   B O D E S   O R T
    E R A     D I G
M A G N E S I A   N O N F A T
C H A R L E S D E G A U L L E
C O M E   S L A V   L I E G E
L Y E S   E M E     T E A
```

PUZZLE 45

PUZZLE 46

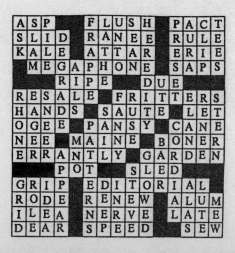

PUZZLE 47

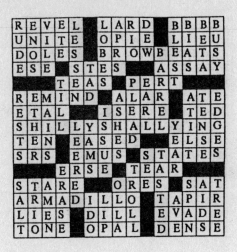

PUZZLE 48

PUZZLE 49

```
S C U D   F A U L T   R I G A
L O S E   E N S U E   E R I N
O M E N   A T O N E   C A R D
P A S T O R S   A T T E N D S
      I F S   A C H E D
S C A N T   T R Y   R E E S E
P A R E   P A C   A S S E T S
A R G   M A C A B R E   R O T
N E U R A L   D O E   T I L E
S T E E R   D E B   C H E E R
      P I T A S   E A R
C A P T A I N   A B R E A S T
D R E I   A C E R B   A S T O
V I A L   R E N T E   T I E S
I D L E   A R C E D   S A P S
```

PUZZLE 50

```
G R A P E   S L A B   S H O P
L A V I N   L A T E   L O N E
I C I E R   I D E A   U R S A
B E D R O O M S   D A M S E L
      C L U E   D E P L E T E
G A V E L S   R O D E O
A B E   S T O A S   S R T A S
S L I P   S A V E R   D A L E
P E N A L   S E D A N   F E E
      R I S E N   R A F T E R
G O A T E E S   K E N O
A M A N D A   M O R N I N G S
M E R E   S O A R   I B E A M
I G O R   O B I E   E L O P E
N A N S   N I N A   S E N S E
```

PUZZLE 51

```
. M T S . M A S K . P A G E S
C U R T . A N N A . R E R A N
A R I A . S T I R . A R O S E
N A P L E S I T A L Y . S E E
S L E E V E . T E E N S . . .
. . . E D I T . A R E N A S
A S S T S . D E B S . V E S T
D A T A . P L A N E . E S T A
E R R S . S E R A . A R S O N
S I E S T A . S I L L . . .
. . S E A L S . I T A L I C
W A S . I M P E R S O N A T E
A X I A L . A R U T . O M E N
G E N R E . R I D E . D A R T
E D G E D . K E E N . E S S .
```

PUZZLE 52

```
A D A M S . P R O M . S L O P
M O I R E . S O U P . P U M A
P U R S E . A S T H M A T I C
S R S . T A L E . A R E T E
. S H A M . M A D E .
S H A P E R . S E E M . D O M
T A R A . T E R R A . O N A
R U B S T H E W R O N G W A Y
A T O . H O N E Y . A S I A
P E R . A M O R . T A V E R N
. E W E R . E A S E .
A I S L E . A L P S . R A H
S T E A D F A S T . E L O P E
H A L T . A L T O . N E V E R
E L L E . N E O N . T I E R S
```

PUZZLE 53

```
. S A M . T R A P . E L A T E
D A D A . O O N A . R O M E O
E L A N . T A N S . A S P E N
M A G I S T R A T E S . U S S
I D E A T E . A D E P T . .
. . A R E S . G R E A S E
L A M A R . M A T E . E T T E
A R A B . R I V E R . V E A L
S A R A . I T E M . T E D D Y
S T A T E D . S P A R . . .
. T E N E T . G E N I A L
R A H . T R A V E R S A B L E
A M O L E . P A R E . P A I N
F I N E R . E L S E . E R A S
T E S T S . S E T S . S S S .
```

PUZZLE 54

```
S T E A M . C I R C . S C A M
A R E N A . O V A L . T A L E
T A K E N . S E M I C O L O N
E M S . N U T S . A R M E D
. . M E S S . S I R E . .
A S H O R E . C A S T . A R E
S E A L . T U L L E . B I S
K I N D H E A R T E D N E S S
E N D . E V I L S . A L E E
D E Y . R E L Y . W A T E R S
. . T A R S . S A N E . .
C A M E L . R I N G . L A P
A B A N D O N E D . L O O S E
P E T E . N O D E . E R A S E
S L A T . E G O S . S A F E R
```

PUZZLE 55

```
G R A M   S T A G E   A D A M
R O L E   H A D E S   L O V E
A B E T   A P O R T   I V E S
D E F E N D S   M E R G E R S
      R O E   B A R O N
C A D E T   F U N   S E N S E
R U E D   J A R   S E D A T E
A R E   D E T E C T S   S O L
G A R R E T   A D S   T A L E
S L E E T   D U E   M I L E R
      D E L E S   P O P
C A B A R E T   S E A S O N S
E L E C   E A S E S   T R O Y
L O S T   R I A N T   E E N S
L E T S   S L O T S   R O O T
```

PUZZLE 56

```
O B O E S   W I M P   O D O R
C A R A T   I C E S   M I M E
T I A R A   P O L I C E M E N
S O L   G L E N   A G E N T
      B E E S   M A M A
D E C A D E   P I L E   B E N
E L L E   S O N A R   E M U
C O U R T M A R T I A L L E D
A P E   R U N T S   A L E E
L E D   I L E S   T A T E R S
      E V E R   E R N E
S L A V E   F L A T   A G E
C A F E T E R I A   L A N A I
A M A N   V A S T   E L T O N
B E R T   E T T E   R A I L S
```

PUZZLE 57

PUZZLE 58

PUZZLE 59

PUZZLE 60

PUZZLE 61

PUZZLE 62

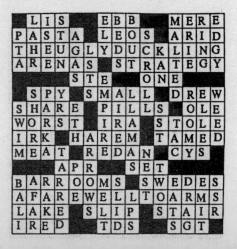

```
JAMES   ZEST   QUAD
UNCLE   ETRE   UNTO
NOISE   ROAR   ATOP
ENVISION   RACINE
    ERNS   MONKEES
MASSED   PUREE
OLE   DICER   WRATH
BOAR   AHEAD   YOKE
SPRAT   ARLES   NOW
    WRAPS   CARESS
AFGHANS   PALE
TULIPS   GALOSHES
ENID   WEAR   OCALA
TONE   ETTE   NUDES
EFTS   REED   SEAMS
```

PUZZLE 64

```
SAND   SLATE   AGRA
ILEA   POISE   ROAD
ATOM   OILER   TONE
MONSOON   TIDINGS
    ELK   USERS
STALE   SSE   OTTER
TOGS   RAH   SPEECH
AXE   DETESTS   PLY
TINTED   RAY   TEAM
ENTER   FEN   CRETE
    EBBED   TAI
MARTYRS   SIMMERS
ALEE   ATILT   MAIL
SOAR   VENAL   ESSE
HEMS   ORATE   DEED
```

PUZZLE 65

```
B R A G   A S A P   H A T E D
R A R E   P E R E   E M O T E
A V O N   O L E O   L O R E N
N E W E N G L A N D E R
      R A E     S U N   R C A
  T R A V E L S   S A B E R S
G R A T E   O U S T   U T A H
R A N I   D O P E S   R E N O
I N T O   I T E R   M E L E E
S C E N I C   R A S C A L S
T E D   D E L   E M U
    P E D I A T R I C I A N
A G O R A   A L A I   R O M E
S A B O T   R O P E   A N E W
S L I M E   S T E S   T A N S
```

PUZZLE 66

```
  A L A   A L L   S T O P
A R O M A   D I A L   P A P A
S A N A N T O N I O T E X A S
S T E N O S   T R A V A I L S
      N A B   D A R
  O D D   R E T I E   S P A T
E M I T S   R I N D S   A R E
T E N S E   A N D   A S S E T
A G E   M A T T E   P A S T E
L A R K   B E S E T   W E E
    A V A   D I N
A M E R I C A N   L E D G E S
S Y R A C U S E N E W Y O R K
K N I T   S E A R   T E R R Y
S A N E   A R A   D E S
```

PUZZLE 67

PUZZLE 68

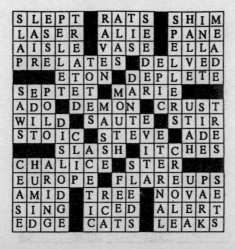

PUZZLE 69

```
O N E     M A J     P E S T
S O A R S   O D O R   O R E O
O Z Z I E A N D H A R R I E T
B E I N G S   S N I C K E R S
      O K S       S A E
  S P A   S E R G E   R A G E
S C E N T   L O R D S   G O D
L E A S H   D U E   E L A T E
I N C   E M O T E   A S T I N
D E E D   A M E N D   T E N
      E R N     S U B
A T H L E T E S   M O L A R S
L E A V E I T T O B E A V E R
A C H E   S O O N   R U I N S
S H A D     N A T   D D T
```

PUZZLE 70

```
V O L S   A D D S   R A N O N
E L I A   D E L L   E M O T E
N E E D   H A V E   C O D E D
D O U B L E D I P P E R
    U A R     T A D   S P A
  B A T T E R Y   P E N C I L
A R E T E   E A S E   O R A L
T E R R   M A N O R   N O N E
B E A U   E L K O   T A L O N
A Z T E C S   S T R O L L S
T E E   A S A     E R I
    P S Y C H O L O G I S T
C O M E T   T U N E   N O P E
A F I R E   E L O N   E T A L
L A X E R   D A R T   D A N E
```

PUZZLE 71

```
  S H E   M C C     P L A N
S A I L S   T H A I   E I R E
P U L L I N G U P S T A K E S
A L L E G E   M E A N N E S S
      N O W     B T U
  P R O   N A T A L   T R A M
L I A N A   V A N E S   E L I
I L I A D   E M S   A B A T E
M A N   S T R E W   D E M O N
P U S S   A S S E T   E S S
      T A N     R A G
A R R A N G E R   N I C H E D
S T A N D O N E S G R O U N D
T E N D   S O D A   L I M I T
A S I S   S O X     L S D
```

PUZZLE 72

```
T R I P   S E P A L   F A D S
H O S E   T R A C Y   A L O E
A M E N   A L T E R   C A R R
T E E N A G E   T E A T I M E
      A P E   D I S C O
C H A N T   D E C   T R E A T
R O U T   D I A   R E S A L E
E R R   S A D D L E D   R O N
A D A P T S   P O X   P E N D
M E L E E   L A G   J A D E S
    T R A I N   M A R
A G A I N S T   F E N C E R S
B O O T   C A R L A   H A I L
L A N E   O N I O N   E S T A
E T E S   T Y P E S   D E E P
```

PUZZLE 73

PUZZLE 74

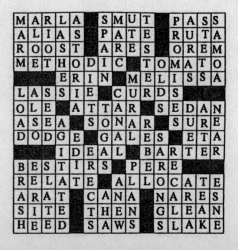

PUZZLE 75

PUZZLE 76

PUZZLE 77

S	A	P	S		R	A	N	C	H		P	R	A	M
T	R	A	P		E	L	O	P	E		R	I	L	E
L	I	R	A		S	T	E	A	M	B	O	A	T	S
O	D	A		U	T	E	S		A	P	S	E	S	
	P	A	R	E	R			E	K	E				
D	O	L	L	A	R		A	V	E	R	S	E		
A	R	E	E	L		L	A	G	E	R		I	S	H
L	A	G	S		L	O	V	E	R		E	L	S	E
E	L	I		B	O	D	E	S		M	A	V	E	N
	S	C	A	R	C	E		H	A	V	E	N	S	
		R	I	O			M	A	T	E	R			
L	I	N	E	D		A	U	S	T		W	E	B	
A	T	O	N	E	M	E	N	T	S		P	A	R	E
L	A	V	A		U	R	K	E	L		U	R	G	E
A	L	A	S		G	R	A	D	E		P	E	O	N

PUZZLE 78

S	I	R		S	C	A	L	E		A	C	T	S	
A	R	A	B		T	O	T	E	M		G	A	I	T
T	A	R	A		A	R	O	S	E		A	G	E	E
	S	A	N	D	P	A	P	E	R		T	E	R	R
		D	I	L	L			A	R	E				
S	T	R	I	V	E		S	A	L	E	S	M	A	N
T	R	I	T	E		C	O	N	D	O		I	D	O
A	I	D	S		D	O	L	E	S		C	L	O	T
I	C	E		R	E	M	O	W		B	L	A	R	E
D	E	R	A	N	G	E	S		P	L	A	N	E	S
		C	A	R			A	R	T	S				
S	L	A	T		A	I	M	L	E	S	S	L	Y	
T	A	R	O		D	R	O	V	E		E	A	S	E
E	M	I	R		E	A	T	I	N		S	T	E	W
P	E	A	S		D	E	A	N	S		E	R	E	

PUZZLE 79

PUZZLE 80

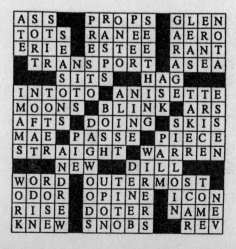

PUZZLE 81

PUZZLE 82

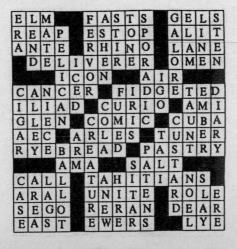

PUZZLE 83

```
C O D E   B R E S T     B L O W
H A R T   A E R I E     R O D E
A S E A   D E S P E R A D O S
P T A   O G L E     A V E R T
    M O D E S     A G O
R U B B E R     C R E S T S
A L O E S   S C A M S   A T O
S T A Y   S T A R S   A B E L
A R T   S P E N T   P L E A D
  A S S E R T     B O A R D S
    A N Y     M O U R N
T O D D S     L O O T   A P T
B R I D E G R O O M   A C R E
A N N A   A N I S E   S L A M
R O O M   P A N E D   H E M P
```

PUZZLE 84

```
  S R S     A C T     M O S S
S L A T S   G A I T   O N U S
T A K E I T O R L E A V E I T
A G E N D A   D E N T I S T S
      E L M     U T E
  A M S   L A S E R   S A R A
S T O P S   S T R E W   L I P
C O R A L   T A R   E R O D E
A N A   O M E G A   D I N E R
B E L T   A R E N T   G E R
    R R S     D E L
T A P I O C A S   C A B A N A
K E E P Y O U R S H I R T O N
O R E L   T R A Y   D O N U T
S O L E   A S S     W O N
```

PUZZLE 85

```
A C T   A P H I D   R I M S
S L A G   P R O S E   E D I T
P A P A   P E A L S   M E T E
  P E R P L E X E S   O A T S
    M I E N     E A T
C O V E T S   M A R V E L E D
O M E N S   C A S T E   O M A
R E N T   P A T H S   T R O T
A G O   D O P E Y   C R E T E
L A M E N T E D   C R A N E S
    A A A     B R A D
L A G S   B E S I E G E R S
A B E T   L I E G E   R O U T
N I N E   E N R O L   S T E R
D E E R   S E A T S   S T Y
```

PUZZLE 86

```
W A F E R   S T A R   E A R P
A M I L E   K I N E   T Z A R
F I N A L   U N I T   E T R E
T E N T A C L E   A G R E E S
  E T A L   F I A N C E S
T E N D E R   M I L L I
A L A   D E P O T   A T L A S
L A M B   S I L L Y   Y I P E
K N E E S   P A Y E E   M E N
  L I V E R   A N G E R S
A S O L D A S   E R S E
B A T H E S   J E N N I F E R
A U T O   T O U R   A G I L E
S T E P   L O N I   R E N E S
H E R S   Y O K E   E R E C T
```

PUZZLE 87

```
P A S S     D A D S     R O P E S
A N T I     I R A N     O V E R T
R O A M     T A T A     M E A N Y
C A R P E T B A G G E R
    L A O       S I R     A P O
  T R E S S E S     R O M P E D
C R A T E     D O L L     A P E D
R E D O     H A L O S     G O R E
A M I N     A M E S     R I S E R
B O O S T S     R E P O S E D
S R S     I T S       R U T
    P R O P R I E T R E S S
M A R I A     R O D E     A A A A
A L O U D     A M E N     T R I M
T E N S E     Y E A S     E N D S
```

PUZZLE 88

```
    S O D     S P A S     L O C A L
A T T U       C O L O     E R O D E
M A T E       E R A L     S A L E S
P R E T E N T I O U S       L S T
S T R O V E       S T E R E
        A S E A     T R E A T S
J A D E S     E L S E     A G E E
A M I D     E N D O R     C U R E
B A S E     A Y E S     S T E R N
S T A M P S     R O L E
    G A L E S       A N S W E R
H U R     E D I T O R S H I P S
O P E R A     L E N D     E L E V
S T E M S     L A C E     B E E P
P O S S E     Y S E R     A S S
```

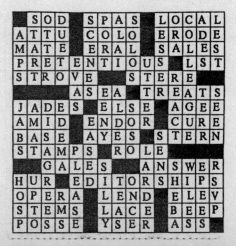

PUZZLE 89

```
T A C O   S A M O A   A M I S
B E A K   A C O R N   V I D A
S I P S   S H O R T F A L L S
P O I   S H E D   R I L E S
  T A P E S   G E L
S L A V E S   P R E S T O
P A L E D   S O R A S   E L M
E M I R   S H R E D   L E D A
W A S   S O O T Y   S I T E S
  S T R A I T   F L O O R S
  A L L   A R E N T
S M O T E   K N O W   A S H
L A V I S H N E S S   O L E O
O R E O   M O N E T   W E L L
T E R N   S T O R Y   E R L E
```